THE TRINITY

A JOURNAL

THE TRINITY

A JOURNAL

Kenneth Boa

NAVPRESS

BRINGING TRUTH TO LIFE

P.O. Box 35001, Colorado Springs, Colorado 80935

The Navigators is an international Christian organization. Our mission is to reach, disciple, and equip people to know Christ and to make Him known through successive generations. We envision multitudes of diverse people in the United States and every other nation who have a passionate love for Christ, live a lifestyle of sharing Christ's love, and multiply spiritual laborers among those without Christ.

NavPress is the publishing ministry of The Navigators. NavPress publications help believers learn biblical truth and apply what they learn to their lives and ministries. Our mission is to stimulate spiritual formation among our readers.

The introductory material in this journal was adapted from the section on devotional spirituality in Kenneth Boa's book, *Conformed to His Image* (Grand Rapids: Zondervan Publishing House, 2001), with permission of the publishers.

© 2001 by Kenneth Boa
All rights reserved. No part of this publication may be reproduced in any form without written permission from NavPress, P.O. Box 35001, Colorado Springs, CO 80935.
www.navpress.com
Library of Congress Catalog Card Number: 00-056875
ISBN 1-57683-250-3

Cover design by Dan Jamison
Cover photo by C. Arend/Alaska Stock
Creative Team: Jacqueline Eaton Blakley, Lori Mitchell, Glynese Northam

Boa, Kenneth.
     The Trinity : a journal ; spiritual formation through personal encounters with scripture / Kenneth Boa.
          p. cm.
     ISBN 1-57683-250-3
          1. Trinity—Prayer books and devotions—English. 2. Spiritual journals—Authorship.
3. Bible—Devotional use. I. Title.
BT111.2 .B58 2001
248.3—dc21

                                                                                00-056875

Printed in the United States of America

1 2 3 4 5 6 7 8 9 10 / 05 04 03 02 01

Inside This Journal

AN INTRODUCTION TO THE TRINITY

OUR IMAGE OF GOD

> *There is but one God, the Father, from whom are all things, and we exist for Him; and one Lord, Jesus Christ, by whom are all things, and we exist through Him.*
>
> —1 Corinthians 8:6

We do not exist for ourselves—we exist *for* the Father and *through* the Son. The world tells us that we derive our existence from it and that we should live for ourselves, but the Word teaches us that all we are and have comes from the Father who formed us for His pleasure and purposes.

Ultimate reality is not the cosmos or a mysterious force, but an infinite and loving Person. The implications of this are astounding and pervasive. The infinite-personal Lord of all is an unbounded loving community of three timeless and perfect Persons. In the superabundance of His joy and life, He is at once solitude and society, the one and the many, supernal being as communion. The magnificent God who abounds in personal plenitude has no needs, yet He invites us to participate in the intense and interpenetrating life of the three eternally subsistent Selves. Jesus prayed on our behalf "that they may all be one; even as You, Father, are in Me and I in You, that they also may be in Us. . . . I in them and You in Me, that they may be perfected in unity, so that the world may know that You sent Me, and loved them, even as You have loved Me" (John 17:21,23). The impenetrable mystery of us being in the divine Us, and the divine Us being in us, transcends our imagination— but if it is true, all else pales in comparison.

Devotional spirituality revels in the glorious attributes of God and aspires to lay hold of God's aspiration for us. It prepares our souls for the "mystic sweet communion" of living entirely in God and in one another as the three Persons of God eternally live and rejoice in one another. It instills in us a passion for Christ's indwelling life and inspires us to swim in the river of torrential love that flows from His throne of grace.

In 1677, Henry Scougal observed in his little book *The Life of God in the Soul of Man* that "The worth and excellency of a soul is to be measured by the object of its love." Our souls become emaciated when their pleasure is affixed to position, possessions, and power, because these things are destined to corrupt and perish. But as we gradually (and often painfully) transfer our affections from the created and finite world to the uncreated and infinite Maker of the world, our souls become great and glorious. As we take the risk of seeking God's pleasure above our own, we discover the ironic byproduct of a greater satisfaction and contentment than if we sought these things as ends in themselves. As we learn to fix our eyes on Jesus, not for His benefits but *for Himself,* we find that we have all things in Him.

Scripture teaches us that we steadily become conformed to what we most love and admire. *We become like our focus;* as we behold the glory of the Lord, we are being "transformed into the same image from glory to glory, just as from the Lord, the Spirit" (2 Corinthians 3:18). We gradually come to resemble what we worship. But if our heart's desire is fixed on something in this world, it becomes idolatrous and soul-corrupting. Hosea declared that the people of Israel "became as detestable as that which they loved" (Hosea 9:10). But when we turn the focus of our love away from the idols of this world system to the beauty of Christ, we discover the liberty of the Spirit of the Lord. If we draw life from loving communion with the caring, radiant, majestic, and unfathomable Being who formed us for Himself, our souls become noble as they grow in conformity to His character.

GOD'S WORLD, HIS WORD, HIS WORKS, AND HIS WAYS

God in His inner essence is a mystery beyond our comprehension; we will never know Him as He knows Himself. The great pilgrims along the way have discovered that progress from superficial to substantive apprehension of God is not so much a movement from darkness to light as it is a plummeting into the ever-increasing profundity of the cloud of unknowing. Kallistos Ware in *The Orthodox Way* distinguishes the *essence* of God and the *energies* of God. In His essence, God is radically transcendent, but in His energies, He is immanent and omnipresent. As Ware notes, "The Godhead is simple and indivisible, and has no parts. The essence signifies the whole God as he is in himself; the energies signify the whole God as he is in action. God in his entirety is completely present in each of his divine energies." As we reflect on the way God reveals Himself, we come to know Him more clearly, and this enables us to love Him more dearly, and to follow Him more nearly. God makes Himself known to us through His world, His Word, His works, and His ways.

Loving God Through His World

> *The heavens are telling of the glory of God; and their expanse is declaring the work of His hands.*
>
> —Psalm 19:1

> *O Lord, how many are Your works! In wisdom You have made them all; the earth is full of Your possessions.*
>
> —Psalm 104:24

Read Psalm 19:1-6 and Psalms 104 and 148 carefully and prayerfully and you will be struck by the manifold ways in which God designed the heavens and earth to display His glory, wisdom, and greatness.

Meditation on the created order is too often neglected as a meaningful component of devotional spirituality. This is unfortunate, because creation abounds with resplendent wonders on every order of magnitude from the microcosm to the macrocosm that point beyond themselves to the beauty and unimaginable brilliance of the Creator of the cosmos. Consider these marvels of order and design: particles and atoms, light and colors, microbes and diatoms, snowflakes, insects, seeds, flowers, leaves, shells, rocks and minerals, fruits, vegetables, plants, small and large birds, small and large fish, whales, small and large animals, trees, mountains, clouds, weather, the seasons, our earth, the planets, stars, nebulae, our galaxy, clusters and super-clusters of galaxies.

> *You formed my inward parts; You wove me in my mother's womb.*
> *I will give thanks to You, for I am fearfully and wonderfully*
> *made; wonderful are Your works, and my soul knows it very well.*
>
> —Psalm 139:13-14

Of all God's created works, the human body best displays God's creative skill and design. I recommend two books that will help you worship God by reflecting on the marvels of the human and spiritual body: *Fearfully and Wonderfully Made* and *In His Image* by Dr. Paul Brand and Philip Yancey. These books portray the way physical systems like cells, bone, skin, motion, blood, the head, and the sensation of pain teach spiritual truth.

Let me mention two things that have helped me love God through His world. The first is an occasional trip to special places where I am encompassed in the natural order. In such places I sometimes sit back and stare at the stars until I realize that I am no longer looking up, but also *down,* and that I am wholly enveloped by the splendor and grandeur of the heavens. An experience like this is humbling because it dramatically shifts my perspective and reminds me that apart from God and His grace, I am nothing. I gain a similar sense of awe by looking at recent photographs of star clouds and distant galaxies. The veritable explosion in scientific knowledge in our time gives us access to new avenues of appreciating God that were never before available.

The second thing I use to stimulate wonder is a set of field lenses and a miniature high-intensity flashlight. I use this "nature kit" from time to time to observe otherwise invisible colors and patterns in flowers, insects, rocks, and so forth. The very act of slowing down enough to observe and appreciate the rich intricacy and diversity of the created order is a healthy exercise in recollection and renewal.

There is no limit to the images and insights that can be gleaned from nature if we take the time and have the eyes to see. We would do well to cultivate a childlike sense of amazement and awe at the things we tend to overlook every day. Our artificial environments and busy schedules make us forget that we are surrounded by mystery and majesty. I encourage you to make the effort to enjoy more frequent and deliberate contact with God's creation and to develop a deeper appreciation for the complexity, beauty, and resplendence of the heavens and the earth. As you do this, you will sense that the God who designed all this and spoke it into being is utterly competent, trustworthy, and lovable.

Loving God Through His Word

> Open my eyes, that I may behold wonderful things from Your law.
> —Psalm 119:18

> The Word of God restores the soul, imparts wisdom, gives joy to the heart, enlightens the eyes, reveals God's righteousness, and endures forever.
> —Psalm 19:7-9

Scripture was revealed not merely to inform us, but to transform us. In *Shaped by the Word*, M. Robert Mulholland Jr. contrasts two approaches to Scripture:

INFORMATIONAL READING	FORMATIONAL READING
Seeks to cover as much as possible	Focuses on small portions
A linear process	An in-depth process
Seeks to master the text	Allows the text to master us
The text as an object to use	The text as a subject that shapes us
Analytical, critical, and judgmental approach	Humble, detached, willing, loving approach
Problem-solving mentality	Openness to mystery

There is an important place for informational reading of Scripture and for exegetical and topical methods of Bible study. But those who approach Scripture only in this way often overlook the formational approach that centers on speaking to the heart more than informing the mind. The Bible is not merely an object, but a divinely inspired oracle that is "living and active" (Hebrews 4:12) and has the power to transform those who receive it in humility and obedience (James 1:21-22). Devotional spirituality stresses the formative power of revealed truth and encourages us to love God through His Word. We will look at a time-tested method of doing this in the pages ahead.

Loving God Through His Works

> Say to God, "How awesome are Your works!"
> Come and see the works of God,
> Who is awesome in His deeds toward the sons of men.
> I shall remember the deeds of the Lord;
> Surely I will remember Your wonders of old.
> I will meditate on all Your work
> And muse on Your deeds.
> You are the God who works wonders;
> You have made known Your strength among the peoples.
> You have by Your power redeemed Your people.
>
> —Psalms 66:3,5; 77:11-12,14-15

The psalmists frequently reviewed and reflected upon God's historical acts of redemption, protection, and provision. Both Testaments abound with accounts of how God has worked in specific and dramatic ways in the lives of people and in the destiny of nations. He has demonstrated His just and loving purposes in the arena of human history, and prayerful consideration of His mighty works of creation, redemption, and consummation is another way of enhancing our worship and devotion for the triune Godhead.

> Worthy are You, our Lord and our God, to receive glory and
> honor and power; for You created all things, and because of Your
> will they existed, and were created. . . . Worthy are You to take
> the book and to break its seals; for You were slain, and purchased
> for God with Your blood men from every tribe and tongue and
> people and nation. You have made them to be a kingdom and
> priests to our God; and they will reign upon the earth. . . .
> Worthy is the Lamb that was slain to receive power and riches
> and wisdom and might and honor and glory and blessing. . . .
> To Him who sits on the throne, and to the Lamb, be blessing and
> honor and glory and dominion forever and ever.
>
> —Revelation 4:11; 5:9-10,12-13

Loving God Through His Ways

> He made known His ways to Moses, His acts to the sons of Israel.
>
> —Psalm 103:7

Moses not only knew the Lord through His works, but he also knew and loved the Lord through His ways. God's ways concern His personal involvement in our lives and our experience of His peace, power, provision, protection, compassion, and care. It is good to build a "personal history" of God's providential care by reviewing and remembering the things He has done at various points along your spiritual journey. Remember His surprising answers to prayer, the way He drew you to Himself, the way He carried you through turbulent waters, the way He provided for your needs when circumstances looked hopeless, the way He encouraged and comforted you in your distress, the way He exhorted you through others and disciplined you for your good, and the way He seeks to strip you of your hope in the things of this world so that you will learn to hope only in Him.

> Come and hear, all who fear God,
> And I will tell of what He has done for my soul.
> Certainly God has heard;
> He has given heed to the voice of my prayer.
> Blessed be God,
> Who has not turned away my prayer
> Nor His lovingkindness from me.
> Your way, O God, is holy;
> What god is great like our God?
>
> —Psalm 66:16,19-20; 77:13

I will tell of what He has done for my soul. Grateful reflection on what God has done for your soul is a vital component of devotional spirituality.

God's ways also relate to the multifaceted attributes of His person, powers, and perfection. Since our capacity to love God is related to our image of God, we do well to pray for the grace of growing in understanding of the glories of His attributes: His unlimited power, presence, and knowledge; His holiness, justice, goodness, truthfulness, and righteousness; His goodness, grace, compassion, mercy, and love; His beauty, glory, greatness, transcendent majesty, and dominion; and His self-existence, eternity, infinity, and immutability. As Dallas Willard puts it in *The Divine Conspiracy,* God is "an interlocking community of magnificent persons, completely self-sufficing and with no meaningful limits on goodness and power." He is the absolute answer to the perennial quest for the true, the good, and the beautiful.

THE PRACTICE OF SACRED READING

The ancient art of sacred reading (*lectio divina*) centers on loving God through His Word. It was introduced to the West by the Eastern desert father John Cassian early in the fifth century. The sixth-century Rule of St. Benedict that guided Benedictine and Cistercian monastic practice prescribed daily periods for sacred reading. Unfortunately, by the end of the Middle Ages it came to be seen as a method that should be restricted to the spiritually elite. As time passed, even monastics lost the simplicity of sacred reading as it was replaced by more complicated systems and forms of "mental prayer." In recent decades, however, this ancient practice has been revitalized, especially by those in the Cistercian tradition. Writers like Thomas Merton (*Contemplative Prayer, New Seeds of Contemplation, Spiritual Direction & Meditation*), Thomas Keating (*Intimacy with God; Open Mind, Open Heart*), Michael Casey (*Sacred Reading, Toward God, The Undivided Heart*), and Thelma Hall (*Too Deep for Words*) have been promoting sacred reading in Catholic circles, and Protestants are now being exposed to this approach as well. Sacred reading, or *lectio divina*, involves a progression through the four movements of reading, meditation, prayer, and contemplation.

READING (*LECTIO*)

In his study of monastic culture, *The Love of Learning and the Desire for God*, Jean Leclercq distinguished two distinct approaches to Scripture that were used in the Middle Ages. While medieval universities were urban schools that prepared clerics for the active life, rural monasteries focused on spiritual formation within a liturgical framework to equip monks for the contemplative life. The scholastics approached Scripture by focusing on the page of sacred text (*sacra pagina*) as an object to be studied and investigated by putting questions to the text (*quaestio*) and by questioning oneself with the subject matter (*disputatio*). By contrast, the monastics approached Scripture through a personal orientation of meditation (*meditatio*) and prayer (*oratio*). While the scholastics sought science and knowledge in the text, the monastics sought wisdom and appreciation. Those in the schools were more oriented to the objective, the theological, and the cognitive; those in the cloisters were more oriented to the subjective, the devotional, and the affective.

Most contemporary approaches to Bible study have more in common with the scholastics than with the monastics. Recalling a distinction we made earlier, they are more concerned with informational reading than with formational reading. There is a legitimate need for both approaches, since an overemphasis on one or the other can lead to the extremes of cold intellectualism or mindless enthusiasm. But when evangelicals study Scripture, they typically look more for precepts and principles than for an encounter with God in the depths of their being. The practice of *lectio divina* can correct this lack of balance, because it stresses the reading of Scripture for spiritual formation through receptive openness to God's loving call of grace. *Lectio* is not an intellectual exercise that seeks to control and to gather information, but a voluntary immersion in the Word of God that seeks to receive and to respond. Spiritual reading melds revelation with experience. It is done in the spirit of the collect for the second Sunday in Advent in the 1928 *Book of Common Prayer:*

Blessed Lord, who hast caused all holy Scriptures to be written for our learning; Grant that we may in such wise hear them, read, mark, learn, and inwardly digest them, that by patience and comfort of thy holy Word, we may embrace, and ever hold fast, the blessed hope of everlasting life, which thou hast given us in our Saviour Jesus Christ.

May we learn to hear the holy Scriptures and to "read, mark, learn, and inwardly digest" them.

Suggestions for Reading

- Choose a special place (preferably away from your desk and other areas of activity) that is suitable for this purpose. Sanctify this space by reserving it as a regular meeting place with the Lord.
- Choose a special time in which you can be alert and consistent. Invite God to lead you to rearrange your life to allow more time with Him. This will be more a matter of *making* time rather than finding time. Making time for this purpose is a response to God's calling in a world of constant external demands. Although this will not work for everyone, I recommend exchanging the last hour of the night for an extra hour in the morning. (Most of us could redeem a significant amount of time by reducing and being more selective in our intake of television.) Whenever it is, give God your best time, when you are least sluggish, and when you can be quiet, still, and unpressured by outward hindrances.
- Consistency is critical, since there will be many temptations to postpone and neglect sacred reading. The benefits of *lectio* are attained gradually over a long-term process.
- Since *lectio divina* engages the whole person, your bodily posture is important. A seated position that is erect but not tense or slouched is best for the four movements of *lectio*. It is good to be fully attentive and alert without sitting in a way that will eventually impede your circulation or breathing.
- Try to be systematic in the way you select your Scripture texts. They can emerge from a daily Bible reading program or through the use of a lectionary that gives you daily Old Testament, gospel, and epistle readings. Or your passages can come out of a devotional guide. (I often use my *Handbook to Prayer* and *Handbook to Renewal* for this purpose.)
- To avoid distraction in sacred reading, it is better to use a Bible without study notes. Use an accurate translation rather than a paraphrase (I use the updated edition of the NASB) for *lectio divina*.
- Keep the passage brief—do not confuse quantity with quality.
- It is also helpful to apply this method of slow, deliberate, and prayerful reading to other resources such as the creeds, traditional and patristic texts, and classic spiritual books. Samples of some of these resources

are available in *Devotional Classics,* edited by Richard J. Foster and James Bryan Smith. Older literature has a way of challenging the biases of our modern presuppositions, if we will let it seep into us.

- Begin with a prayer of preparation: for example, "Open my eyes, that I may behold wonderful things from Your law" (Psalm 119:18), or "Let the words of my mouth and the meditation of my heart be acceptable in Your sight, O Lord, my Rock and my Redeemer" (Psalm 19:14). Start with a clear intention to know God's will for your life and a fixed resolution in advance to do it.

- Slowly read the text again and again until it is in your short-term memory. Try making your first readings audible, since this will make them slower and more deliberate. (Bear in mind that in antiquity, reading always meant reading aloud.)

- Seek the meaning of the text; ask questions. But come more as a disciple than as a collector of information. See Scripture as iconographic; that is, a verbal window into the reality of life that turns your perspective around.

- Listen to the words in humility accompanied by a willingness to obey. Hearing the Word must be united by faith (Hebrews 4:2) with an intention to apply it in practice (James 1:22). Open yourself to be addressed by the Word in your attitudes, habits, choices, and emotions. There will be times when you resist a penetrating living encounter with God, and these generally have to do with areas of disobedience. Thus, it is wise to examine your being and doing in the light of the text by asking, *Lord, what are You saying to me in this passage?*

- Remember that unlike ordinary reading, in *lectio* you are seeking to be *shaped* by the Word more than *informed* by the Word. This first step of reading prepares you for the remaining three movements of meditation, prayer, and contemplation. But the whole process should be infused with a prayerful attitude.

- Avoid the usual pragmatic reflex that seeks to "net out" some immediate benefit. Approach sacred reading with no conditions, demands, or expectations. The Word may not meet your perceived needs, but it will touch your real needs, even when you don't discern them.

MEDITATION (MEDITATIO)

As you move from reading to meditation, you are seeking to saturate and immerse yourself in the Word, to luxuriate in its living waters, and to receive the words as an intimate and personal message from God. The purpose of meditation is to penetrate the Scriptures and to let them penetrate us through the loving gaze of the heart. The term *mental prayer* is often associated with meditation, but this could be misleading, since *lectio, meditatio,* and *oratio* involve not only the mind, but also the heart. Meditation attunes the inward self to the Holy Spirit so that our hearts harmonize and resonate with His voice. Meditation is a spiritual work of holy desire and an interior invitation for the Spirit to pray and speak within us (Romans 8:26-27) in such a way that our whole being is transformed into greater conformity with Jesus Christ. It is an intentional process of building our passion for Christ by meeting with Him and spending time with Him to know Him more clearly, to love Him more dearly, and to follow Him more nearly. By meditating on God's truth, we are inviting Christ to be formed in us (Galatians 4:19) by a deliberate dwelling on His words. Thus, mental prayer should not be seen as an abstract exercise but as a vital vehicle for the metamorphosis of the soul.

> *This book of the law shall not depart from your mouth, but you shall meditate on it day and night, so that you may be careful to do according to all that is written in it; for then you will make your way prosperous, and then you will have success.*
>
> —Joshua 1:8

This familiar verse tells us that the path to success *as God defines it* is the habit of making space in our lives to meet with God in His holy Word with a heartfelt intention to apply what He reveals through obedient action. Only those who delight in God's Word and habitually meditate on it (Psalm 1:2) will experience the fullness and stability of God's purpose and calling. May you be one of them.

Suggestions for Meditation

- Since it is God's love for us that teaches us to love Him, we should not regard meditation as an objective method or technique, but as a person-specific process. It is good to experiment with different approaches until you find a pattern of meditation that resonates best with your soul.
- Acknowledge the holiness of the God you are approaching and the richness of the gift of faith that makes it possible for you to enjoy an encounter with Him through His Spirit.
- Meditation is a long-term process that builds upon itself. The more we absorb Scripture, the greater our mental storehouse becomes. As this process continues for months and years, we experience the phenomenon of *reminiscence* in which a word or phrase spontaneously evokes a wealth of imagery from other parts of Scripture. This can be an exciting and creative experience in which we see connections and rhythms we never perceived before. These chain reactions, the fruit of habitual meditation, develop "the mind of Christ" in us (1 Corinthians 2:16).
- Allow enough time to enjoy the text; to rush this process is like running through a great art gallery.
- Meditation on Scripture involves ruminating *(ruminatio)* on a word, phrase, passage, or story. When we chew on the text in our minds, we

release the full flavor as we assimilate its content.

- Don't force meditation or make impatient demands of immediate gratification and results. Meditation will do you little good if you try to control the outcome.
- When you encounter something that speaks particularly to you, you should note it so that you can reflect on it later. You may find it helpful to make written reminders that you can carry with you.
- It may also be beneficial to keep a journal of your personal reflections on the text. If you do this, you will need to be open and honest with yourself in the things you record. The advantage of a journal is the creation of a private record that can be reviewed from time to time.
- Personalize the words of the text and "real-ize" them; receive them as God speaking to you in the present moment. Try to hear the passage as though for the first time, personally addressed to you.
- When a passage speaks to you, consider meditating on the same text for several days before moving on to another.
- The millions of images we have been exposed to through television, movies, magazines, newspapers, and other media have not sharpened but dulled our creative imagination. More than ever, we need to develop and sanctify our imagination, because the truth of Scripture and spiritual experience is, to use Jean Leclercq's words, "impregnated with a mysterious light impossible to analyze." A sanctified imagination will enable us to grasp more than we can see, but we need the lifeline of Scripture to tether us to the truth.
- Many people have found it helpful to engage the five senses when meditating on biblical stories, especially the stories in the Gospels. This process makes the scene more present and real to us and it helps us transition from the cognitive, analytical level to the affective, feeling level of our being.
- In addition to the imaginative use of the senses, it can be illuminating to put yourself in the story. How would you have reacted, and what would you have thought and said if you were there?
- The *Spiritual Exercises* of Ignatius of Loyola incorporates these and other meditative techniques and has useful insights on contemplating the incarnation, life, death, resurrection, and ascension of Christ. The various meditations and prayers prescribed in *Introduction to the Devout Life* by Francis de Sales (on such topics as our creation, the end for which we were created, sin, death, humility, and God's love for us) are also valuable resources for many. But because temperaments differ, not everyone will find such methodical meditation schemes helpful. Most people are sensory, but some are more analytical, and others are more intuitive. Intuitives will benefit more from savoring the truths of a passage than from its imagery. To quote Dom Chapman, "Pray as you can, not as you can't!"

- Meditation on the Psalms (*meditatio psalmorum*) has edified the saints for thousands of years and should be a regular part of our spiritual diet. It is enormously beneficial in all seasons and conditions of life to savor and absorb the meaning of the Psalms in the depths of one's heart.
- Ideally, meditation should address the mind, the emotions, and the will. Ruminating on Scripture stimulates our thinking and understanding and it also elevates the affections of the heart. It reaches the will when we resolve to let the passage shape our actions. Intellect, imagination, and volition should not be divorced from one another.
- Accept the fact that you will often encounter problems with distraction and inattention. Do not be disturbed when your mind wanders, but gently and calmly return to the text before you. As Thomas Merton stated in *New Seeds of Contemplation,* "It is much better to desire God without being able to think clearly of Him, than to have marvelous thoughts about Him without desiring to enter into union with His will." Normally, it is best to resist the temptation to be distracted by practical concerns, but sometimes it can be helpful to turn these concerns into subjects of meditation in light of the truth of the text.
- Remember that meditation does not need to produce evident affection or consolation in order to be beneficial. The quest for moving experiences can lead to the self-deception of emotional melodrama and counterfeit mysticism.

PRAYER (ORATIO)

The discipline of prayer is usually associated with a personal dialogue (colloquy) with God, though the majority of our prayers appear to be petitionary monologues. In *lectio divina,* prayer is specifically related to the two prior movements of sacred reading and meditation on the text. *Oratio* is the fruit of *meditatio,* and it is the way we "interiorize" what God has spoken to us through the passage. The transition from meditation to prayer may be subtle or unnoticed, but it is a response of the heart to what has been largely occupying the mind. It is a movement from truth to implication, from hearing to acknowledgment, from understanding to obedience.

Depending on how the living and active Word is shaping us (Hebrews 4:12), this period of prayer can be sweet and consoling, or it can be painful and revealing. The two-edged sword of the Spirit has a way of exposing the thoughts and intentions of the heart, and when our selfish, distorted, and manipulative strategies are "open and laid bare to the eyes of Him with whom we have to do" (Hebrews 4:13), *oratio* becomes a time for compunction, confession, and repentance. When the soul is exposed and we see our interior and exterior lives as God sees them, it can be both devastating (in light of God's holiness) and exhilarating (in light of God's forgiveness and compassion). At other times, we may be gripped by the power of spiritual truth (for example, the kindness and love of the Father, the grace and faithfulness of the Son, the fellowship and presence of the Spirit) and respond in adoration or thanksgiving. *Oratio* is a time for participation in the interpenetrating subjectivity of the Trinity through prolonged mutual presence and growing identification with the life of Christ.

Suggestions for Prayer

- Allow enough time so that you do not rush the process; you are not likely to listen to God when you are in a hurry.
- Avoid the rut of reducing this period of prayer to a technique or a routine.
- In *lectio divina,* there is a temptation to substitute reading for prayer. It is helpful to view your reading and meditation on the text as preparation for a personal prayerful response.
- Do not seek to control the content or outcome of your prayer.
- Remember that *oratio* is a time for heart response as you move from the mind to the will. Prayer embraces the practical consequences of the truth you have seen and endeavors to direct your life in accordance with it.
- Depending on your reading and meditation, your response can take a number of different forms, including adoration, confession, renewal, petition, intercession, affirmation, and thanksgiving. All of these are different ways of calling upon the Lord, but at one time a prayer of adoration may be appropriate, while at another time the Spirit may lead you in a prayer of confession or petition.
- When the Lord speaks to you in the text by way of exhortation or encouragement, it is good to "pray it through"—that is, to take the time to internalize the message.
- See this time as an opportunity to move away from your false self (the flesh) toward your true self in Christ.
- Scripture is God-breathed and "profitable for teaching, for reproof, for correction, for training in righteousness" (2 Timothy 3:16). Invite the Spirit to search, teach, encourage, comfort, and correct you. Let Him reveal and dispel your illusions, pride, self-centeredness, stubbornness, ungodly attitudes and habits, stinginess, lack of gratitude, manipulation and control, and so forth.
- Prayer can occur at any time during the *lectio* process, and you may find yourself alternating between reading, meditation, and prayer. *Lectio divina* is not a lockstep, sequential movement.
- When you are distracted, simply return to the text to refocus your attention. Teresa of Avila used an image of prayer as a small fire that occasionally needs to be fed by adding a twig or two. A twig is a few words from Scripture, but too many words become branches that could extinguish the fire.
- Bear in mind that in *lectio divina,* prayer is part of the path that leads to contemplation.

CONTEMPLATION (*CONTEMPLATIO*)

Some who use the term *lectio divina* limit it primarily to slow, careful, and prayerful reading of a biblical passage, book, or other spiritual text rather than the whole movement from reading to meditation to prayer to contemplation. As I see it, however, the process of *lectio divina* should begin with reading and culminate in contemplation. Contemplation is often confused with meditation, but as we will see, they are not synonymous.

Meditation and the prayer that flows out of it bring us into communication with the living and transcendent Lord, and as such they prepare us for contemplation. Meditative prayer should be more than an intellectual exercise; when it is accompanied by affective intention it leads to the love and communion of contemplative prayer. Because of its very nature, it is notoriously difficult to communicate the characteristics of contemplative prayer. It is a mysterious territory in which the language is silence and the action is receptivity. True contemplation is a theological grace that cannot be reduced to logical, psychological, or aesthetic categories. Perhaps these general contrasts between meditative and contemplative prayer will help:

MEDITATIVE PRAYER	CONTEMPLATIVE PRAYER
Speech	Silence
Activity	Receptivity
Discursive thought	Loss of mental images and concepts
Vocal and mental prayer	Wordless prayer and interior stillness
Natural faculties of reason and imagination	Mysterious darkening of the natural faculties
Affective feelings	Loss of feelings
Reading and reflection	Inability to meditate
Doing	Being
Seeking	Receiving
Talking to Jesus	Entering into the prayer of Jesus

When he witnessed the miracle of the transfiguration of Jesus on the holy mountain, the awestruck Peter inappropriately broke into speech and was silenced by the voice out of the cloud that said, "This is My beloved Son, with whom I am well pleased; listen to Him!" (Matthew 17:4-5). When we enter into the numinous territory of contemplation, it is best for us to stop talking and "listen to Him" in simple and loving attentiveness. In this strange and holy land we must remove the sandals of our ideas, constructs, and inclinations, and quietly listen for the voice of God. Periods of contemplation can be little "dark nights of faith." During these times, God may seem absent and silent, but His presence and speech is on a deeper level than what we can feel or understand. By preparing a peaceful place in the soul we learn to "rest in the Lord and wait patiently for Him" (Psalm 37:7).

A number of people have been exposed to aspects of contemplative prayer through *centering prayer,* a practice that was recently revived and updated by three Cistercian monks—Thomas Keating, William Meninger, and Basil Pennington. This method of prayer is based on the fourteenth-century classic of mystical theology *The Cloud of Unknowing.* Another approach to contemplative prayer is the *prayer of the heart* that is described in the *Philokalia,* an anthology of quotations from Eastern monastic Fathers from the third century to the Middle Ages. In this tradition, the invocation of the name of the Lord Jesus is used to create a state of receptivity and interior recollection of the presence of God.

Suggestions for Contemplation

- Take enough time to present yourself before God in silence and yield-edness. Contemplative prayer involves the development of a deeper and more intuitive form of receptivity to the supernatural.
- As with meditation and prayer, do not be concerned with results, feel-ings, or experiences during contemplation. The important thing is to "appear before God" in a quiet and receptive mode of being.
- It is helpful to think of a word or an image that expresses what I call the *spirit of the passage* that you have been processing in your reading, meditation, and prayer. When your mind wanders during your time for contemplation, center yourself by returning once again to the spirit of the passage.
- Contemplation is a gift very few believers have attempted to develop. Expect that growth in this new terrain will involve time, discipline, and the frustration of apparent failure. Don't allow distractions or lack of initial benefits to dissuade you from this time-tested discipline. True contemplation may require years of fidelity, but any consistency in this practice will greatly reward you.
- Contemplation is especially difficult for more extroverted and sensory temperaments. This is a discipline of silence, of loss of control, of aban-doning the attempt to analyze and intellectualize, and of developing the intuitive faculties.
- Remember that you cannot engage in contemplative prayer by your own effort; it is God's work, and it requires a *receptive passivity.* In contemplation it is best to abandon self-consciousness and to allow yourself to be drawn into the inexpressible depths of God's love.
- Because *lectio divina* is not a rigid movement through four steps, you may find yourself going back to reading, meditation, or prayer and returning again to the interior silence of contemplation. The amount of time you spend in each of these four elements is up to you, and you should experiment with this. However, I recommend that you

21

practice all four since each of them has a unique benefit.

- Nourish your interior life by reducing your exposure to radio, television, and other forms of distraction and commotion.

My colleague George Grove uses the following set of analogies to integrate the four components of sacred reading:

LECTIO	MEDITATIO	ORATIO	CONTEMPLATIO
Read	Meditate	Pray	Abide
Lips	Mind	Heart	Spirit
Seek	Find	Knock	Open
Food	Chew	Savor	Fill

Lectio divina engages the whole person, from the physical to the psychological to the inward spiritual center of our being. It promotes a harmonious unity through an organic process that uses a variety of means. Fidelity and consistency in this long-term activity will gradually enhance and enrich your life.

Suggestions for Sacred Reading As a Whole

- Do not reduce sacred reading to a technique, system, or program. It has been called a *methodless method* that contributes to the development of a mode of being toward God. It is a personal process that cultivates a spiritual outlook of trust, receptivity, expectation, worship, and intimacy with God.
- Always see yourself as a beginner in the sense that you never "master" this process. There is always more than we think. Remember that discipline and devotion reinforce each other.
- Feel free to adapt this spiritual formation approach to your temperament. More extroverted people, for example, will only be comfortable with short sessions, while more introverted people will tend to take more time in this process.
- Perhaps the most important suggestion I can make is for you to write out the verse or verses you have used for sacred reading on a given day and carry this card with you through your activities. By doing this, you are making that day's passage your theme for twenty-four hours and using it as a tool to practice the presence of Christ. These cards can also assist you in memorization by moving the texts from short-term to longer-term memory.
- It is possible for some personality types to develop a false supernaturalism by becoming immersed in an artificial experience. Thinking they are communing with God, they are really lost in themselves. This problem of self-delusion and misguided zeal can be corrected by a

willingness to accept sound advice through spiritual direction.

- To aspire to contemplation without cultivating compassion for others is to miss the point and purpose of contemplative prayer. The byproduct of devotional spirituality should always be an increased capacity to love and serve others. By the same token, a growing realization of our union with others in Christ will enhance our capacity to know God.

A BLEND OF CONTEMPLATION AND ACTION

The polarity between the contemplative life and the active life has been a source of tension for many centuries. Saint Gregory advocated a more contemplative approach to prayer as rest from exterior action in the quest for communion with God. Saint Basil promoted a more active approach to prayer in association with work. Carried too far, the contemplative extreme could divorce our primary calling to know God from our secondary calling to express this knowledge in the world. On the other hand, the active extreme tends to elevate our secondary calling of work to the point of replacing our primary calling. A more balanced approach integrates and honors both callings and unites the contemplative and active vocations. Saint Benedict encouraged this blended rhythm of rest and action, interior aspiration and exterior obedience, devotion and discipline, prayer and labor, desire for God and service of neighbor, the spring of living water and the stream that flows out of it. By uniting the strengths of both Mary and Martha, we can learn to be contemplatives in action.

CULTIVATING A PASSION FOR CHRIST

Devotional spirituality is like a delicate grapevine that flourishes only when it is planted in the right soil and carefully cultivated in a good climate. Unless it is nurtured, it will wither from neglect and fail to bear fruit. The fruit of spiritual passion can be threatened by natural enemies, but it can also be stimulated by several sources.

Enemies of Spiritual Passion

- *Unresolved areas of disobedience.* Resisting the prodding of God in an area of your life may seem subtle, but it can be a more serious grievance to the heart of God than we suppose. It is good to invite the Holy Spirit to reveal any barriers in our relationship with God or people that have been erected by sinful attitudes and actions. When these become evident, deal with them quickly and trust in the power of God's forgiveness through the blood of Christ.
- *Complacency.* Without holy desire we will succumb to the sin of spiritual *acedia:* indifference, apathy, and boredom. People who lose the sharp edge of intention and calling can slip into a morass of listlessness and feelings of failure. We must often ask God for the grace of

acute desire so that we will hunger and thirst for Him.

- *Erosion in spiritual disciplines.* Complacency can cause or be caused by a failure to train and remain disciplined in the spiritual life. There are several biblical figures like King Asa (2 Chronicles 14–16) who illustrate the problem of starting well in the first half of life and finishing poorly in the last half. When spiritual disciplines begin to erode, spiritual passion declines as well.
- *External obedience.* There are many people who are more concerned about conformity to rules, moral behavior, and duty than they are about loving Jesus. External obedience without inward affection falls short of the biblical vision of obeying God from the heart (Jeremiah 31:33; Romans 6:17; Ephesians 6:6).
- *Loving truth more than Christ.* Some students of the Word have come to love the content of truth in the Bible more than the Source of that truth. Biblical and systematic theology are worthy of pursuit, but not when they become substitutes for the pursuit of knowing and becoming like Jesus.
- *Elevating service and ministry above Christ.* It is easier to define ourselves by what we accomplish than by our new identity in Christ. For some, the Christian life consists more of fellowship, service to those in need, witnessing, and worship than of becoming intimate with Jesus. This leads to the problem of ministry without the manifest presence of God.
- *Greater commitment to institutions than to Christ.* It is easy for churches, denominations, or other organizations to occupy more of our time and attention than devotion to Jesus. There is a constant danger of getting more passionate about causes than about Christ.
- *A merely functional relationship.* Many people are more interested in what Jesus can do for them than in who He is. We may initially come to Him hoping that He will help us with our career, marriage, children, or health, but if we do not grow beyond this "gifts above the Giver" mentality, we will never develop spiritual passion.

Sources of Spiritual Passion

- *Growing awareness of God as a Person.* God is an intensely personal and relational Being, and it is an insult for us to treat Him as though He were a power or a principle. Some of us find it easier to be comfortable with abstract principles and ideas than with people and intimacy. As we have seen, good things like the Bible, theology, ministry, and church can become substitutes for loving Him. As a countermeasure, it is good to ask God for the grace of increased passion for His Son so that, by the power of the Spirit, we will come to love Him as the Father loves Him.
- *Sitting at Jesus' feet.* When we make consistent time for reading, meditation, prayer, and contemplation, we place ourselves at the feet of

Jesus and enjoy His presence. By making ourselves available and receptive to Him, we learn the wisdom of spending more time being a friend of Jesus than a friend of others.

- *Imitating the Master.* Our identification with Jesus in His death, burial, resurrection, and ascension has made us new creatures before God (2 Corinthians 5:17). This divinely wrought identification makes it possible for us to imitate Jesus and "follow in His steps" (1 Peter 2:21). If we love the Master, we will want to be like Him in His character, humility, compassion, love, joy, peace, and dependence on the Father's will.

- *Cultivating spiritual affections.* Regardless of our natural temperaments, it is important for us to develop true affections (desire, longing, zeal, craving, hunger) for God. The rich emotional life of the psalmists (see Psalm 27:4; 42:1-3; 63:1-8; 145:1-21) reveals a desire for God above all else and a willingness to cling to Him during times of aridity and dryness. Like them, we must aspire to a love that is beyond us (Ephesians 3:17-19).

- *Increasing appreciation for the goodness of God.* The distractions of the world make it difficult for us to develop a growing appreciation for our relationship with God. We forget that we can enjoy communion with Someone who is infinitely better than the objects of our most powerful natural desires. We must pray for the grace of gratitude and amazement at the unqualified goodness of God's "kindness toward us in Christ Jesus" (Ephesians 2:7).

- *Focused intention.* What do you want (or want to want) more than anything else? God is pleased when we pursue Him with a heart that is intent on knowing and loving Him. He "begins His influence by working in us that we may have the will, and He completes it by working with us when we have the will" (Augustine, *On Grace and Free Will*). As our wills become more simplified and centered on becoming like Jesus, our love for Him will grow.

- *Willingness to let God break the outward self.* "Unless a grain of wheat falls into the earth and dies, it remains alone; but if it dies, it bears much fruit. He who loves his life loses it, and he who hates his life in this world will keep it to life eternal" (John 12:24-25). The alabaster vial of the self-life must be broken (Mark 14:3) to release the perfume of the new self in Christ. If we wish to manifest the fragrance of Christ, we must allow God to bring us (in His time and way) to the painful place of brokenness on the cross of self-abandonment to Him. This theme resonates in spiritual literature, and one of the clearest expressions is in Watchman Nee's *The Release of the Spirit*.

- *Desiring to please God more than to impress people.* If we want to be like Christ, we must embrace His governing goal to be pleasing to the Father (John 8:29; Hebrews 10:7). The enemy of this glorious goal is the competing quest for human approval (John 5:41,44; 12:43;

Galatians 1:10). We cannot have it both ways; we will either play to an Audience of One or to an audience of many. But in the end, only God's opinion will matter.

- *Treasuring God.* Dallas Willard observes in *The Divine Conspiracy* that God "treasures those whom he has created, planned for, longed for, sorrowed over, redeemed, and befriended." Just as God has treasured us, so He wants us to respond by treasuring Him above all else. "We love, because He first loved us" (1 John 4:19)—the more we realize how God loved and valued us, the greater our capacity to love and value Him. In *Beginning to Pray,* Anthony Bloom suggests that one way to treasure God is to find a personal name or expression for God that flows out of our relationship with him, like David's "You, my Joy!"
- *Maturing in trust.* As believers, we trust Christ for our eternal destiny, but most of us find it difficult to trust Him in our daily practice. As long as we pursue sinful strategies of seeking satisfaction on our own terms, our confidence will be misplaced. We must learn to trust Jesus enough to place our confidence in His power, not in our performance.

GETTING THE MOST OUT OF THIS JOURNAL

This is one of four journals in the *Reflections* series, and it is designed to guide you through three months of sacred reading passages. I have selected ninety texts from Scripture that are particularly well suited to the process of sacred reading to take you on a meditative journey through each of the three Persons of the divine Trinity. This journal provides you with thirty passages on the Father, thirty passages on the Son, and thirty passages on the Holy Spirit. These texts range from one to several verses, and they are arranged in biblical sequence. I have translated the verses from the original languages, and in several cases I have adapted and personalized these passages.

The daily four-part sequence of reading, meditation, prayer, and contemplation invites you to engage personally with the text and to record your thoughts and prayers in the process. This journaling component will enhance your interaction with each of the readings, and it will yield a valuable record of your reflections and prayers during these months. When you have completed this journal of sacred readings, you will profit from reading through the comments and prayers you have recorded.

I also suggest you go through this process a second time and visit each of these passages once again. You will discover new things in the Scripture texts that you did not see the first time through.

*May the God of our Lord Jesus Christ, the Father of glory, give
you a spirit of wisdom and of revelation in the full knowledge of
Him, and may the eyes of your heart be enlightened, in order that
you may know what is the hope of His calling, what are the
riches of His glorious inheritance in the saints, and what is the
incomparable greatness of His power toward us who believe.*

—Ephesians 1:17-19

*O my soul, above all things and in all things always rest in the
Lord, for He is the eternal rest of the saints.*

*Grant me most sweet and loving Jesus, to rest in You above
every other creature, above all health and beauty, above all glory
and honor, above all power and dignity, above all knowledge and
precise thought, above all wealth and talent, above all joy and
exultation, above all fame and praise, above all sweetness and
consolation, above all hope and promise, above all merit and
desire, above all gifts and favors You give and shower upon me,
above all happiness and joy that the mind can understand and
feel, and finally, above all angels and archangels, above all the
hosts of heaven, above all things visible and invisible, and above
all that is not You, my God.*

—Thomas à Kempis, *The Imitation of Christ*

SCRIPTURE

You are the Lord, the God of our fathers—the God of Abraham, the God of Isaac, and the God of Jacob. This is Your name forever, the name by which You are to be remembered from generation to generation. (Exodus 3:15)

READING

Slowly read the Scripture passage several times.

MEDITATION

Take some time to reflect on the words and phrases in the text. Which words, phrases, or images speak most to you?

PRAYER

Offer the internalized passage back to God in the form of a personalized prayer of adoration, confession, renewal, petition, intercession, affirmation, or thanksgiving.

CONTEMPLATION

What word or image captures the spirit of the passage for you?

Take a few minutes to present yourself before God in silence and yieldedness. When your mind wanders, center yourself by returning to the spirit of the passage.

SCRIPTURE

Who is like You, O Lord? Who is like You—majestic in holiness,
awesome in praises, working wonders? (Exodus 15:11)

READING

Slowly read the Scripture passage several times.

MEDITATION

Take some time to reflect on the words and phrases in the text.
Which words, phrases, or images speak most to you?

PRAYER

Offer the internalized passage back to God in the form of a personalized
prayer of adoration, confession, renewal, petition, intercession,
affirmation, or thanksgiving.

CONTEMPLATION

What word or image captures the spirit of the passage for you?

Take a few minutes to present yourself before God in silence and
yieldedness. When your mind wanders, center yourself by returning
to the spirit of the passage.

SCRIPTURE

The Lord is a jealous God, punishing the children for the sin of the fathers to the third and fourth generation of those who hate Him, but showing lovingkindness to a thousand generations of those who love Him and keep His commandments. (Exodus 20:5-6; Deuteronomy 5:9-10)

READING

Slowly read the Scripture passage several times.

MEDITATION

Take some time to reflect on the words and phrases in the text.
Which words, phrases, or images speak most to you?

PRAYER

Offer the internalized passage back to God in the form of a personalized prayer of adoration, confession, renewal, petition, intercession, affirmation, or thanksgiving.

CONTEMPLATION

What word or image captures the spirit of the passage for you?

Take a few minutes to present yourself before God in silence and yieldedness. When your mind wanders, center yourself by returning to the spirit of the passage.

SCRIPTURE

God is not a man, that He should lie, nor a son of man, that He should change His mind. Has He spoken and not done it? Has He promised and not fulfilled it? (Numbers 23:19)

READING

Slowly read the Scripture passage several times.

MEDITATION

Take some time to reflect on the words and phrases in the text.
Which words, phrases, or images speak most to you?

PRAYER

Offer the internalized passage back to God in the form of a personalized prayer of adoration, confession, renewal, petition, intercession, affirmation, or thanksgiving.

CONTEMPLATION

What word or image captures the spirit of the passage for you?

Take a few minutes to present yourself before God in silence and yieldedness. When your mind wanders, center yourself by returning to the spirit of the passage.

SCRIPTURE

The Lord my God is God of gods and Lord of lords, the great God, mighty and awesome, who shows no partiality and accepts no bribes. He executes justice for the fatherless and the widow and loves the alien, giving him food and clothing. (Deuteronomy 10:17-18)

READING

Slowly read the Scripture passage several times.

MEDITATION

Take some time to reflect on the words and phrases in the text. Which words, phrases, or images speak most to you?

PRAYER

Offer the internalized passage back to God in the form of a personalized prayer of adoration, confession, renewal, petition, intercession, affirmation, or thanksgiving.

CONTEMPLATION

What word or image captures the spirit of the passage for you?

Take a few minutes to present yourself before God in silence and yieldedness. When your mind wanders, center yourself by returning to the spirit of the passage.

SCRIPTURE

You are the living God, and there is no god besides You. You put to death and You bring to life, You have wounded and You will heal, and no one can deliver from Your hand. (Deuteronomy 32:39)

READING

Slowly read the Scripture passage several times.

MEDITATION

Take some time to reflect on the words and phrases in the text. Which words, phrases, or images speak most to you?

PRAYER

Offer the internalized passage back to God in the form of a personalized prayer of adoration, confession, renewal, petition, intercession, affirmation, or thanksgiving.

CONTEMPLATION

What word or image captures the spirit of the passage for you?

Take a few minutes to present yourself before God in silence and yieldedness. When your mind wanders, center yourself by returning to the spirit of the passage.

SCRIPTURE

The Lord brings death and makes alive; He brings down to the grave and raises up. The Lord sends poverty and wealth; He humbles and He exalts. He raises the poor from the dust and lifts the needy from the ash heap, to seat them with princes and make them inherit a throne of honor. For the foundations of the earth are the Lord's, and He has set the world upon them. (1 Samuel 2:6-8)

READING

Slowly read the Scripture passage several times.

MEDITATION

Take some time to reflect on the words and phrases in the text. Which words, phrases, or images speak most to you?

PRAYER

Offer the internalized passage back to God in the form of a personalized prayer of adoration, confession, renewal, petition, intercession, affirmation, or thanksgiving.

CONTEMPLATION

What word or image captures the spirit of the passage for you?

Take a few minutes to present yourself before God in silence and yieldedness. When your mind wanders, center yourself by returning to the spirit of the passage.

SCRIPTURE

O Lord, God of Israel, there is no God like You in heaven above or on earth below; You keep Your covenant and mercy with Your servants who walk before You with all their heart. (1 Kings 8:23; 2 Chronicles 6:14)

READING

Slowly read the Scripture passage several times.

MEDITATION

Take some time to reflect on the words and phrases in the text. Which words, phrases, or images speak most to you?

PRAYER

Offer the internalized passage back to God in the form of a personalized prayer of adoration, confession, renewal, petition, intercession, affirmation, or thanksgiving.

CONTEMPLATION

What word or image captures the spirit of the passage for you?

Take a few minutes to present yourself before God in silence and yieldedness. When your mind wanders, center yourself by returning to the spirit of the passage.

SCRIPTURE

The Lord is great and greatly to be praised; He is to be feared above all gods. For all the gods of the nations are idols, but the Lord made the heavens. Splendor and majesty are before Him; strength and joy are in His place. I will ascribe to the Lord glory and strength. I will ascribe to the Lord the glory due His name and worship the Lord in the beauty of holiness. (1 Chronicles 16:25-29)

READING

Slowly read the Scripture passage several times.

MEDITATION

Take some time to reflect on the words and phrases in the text.
Which words, phrases, or images speak most to you?

PRAYER

Offer the internalized passage back to God in the form of a personalized prayer of adoration, confession, renewal, petition, intercession, affirmation, or thanksgiving.

CONTEMPLATION

What word or image captures the spirit of the passage for you?

Take a few minutes to present yourself before God in silence and yieldedness. When your mind wanders, center yourself by returning to the spirit of the passage.

SCRIPTURE

Yours, O Lord, is the greatness and the power and the glory and the victory and the majesty, for everything in heaven and earth is Yours. Yours, O Lord, is the kingdom, and You are exalted as head over all. Both riches and honor come from You, and You are the ruler of all things. In Your hand is power and might to exalt and to give strength to all. Therefore, my God, I give You thanks and praise Your glorious name. All things come from You, and I can only give You what comes from Your hand.
(1 Chronicles 29:11-14)

READING

Slowly read the Scripture passage several times.

MEDITATION

Take some time to reflect on the words and phrases in the text.
Which words, phrases, or images speak most to you?

PRAYER

Offer the internalized passage back to God in the form of a personalized prayer of adoration, confession, renewal, petition, intercession, affirmation, or thanksgiving.

CONTEMPLATION

What word or image captures the spirit of the passage for you?

Take a few minutes to present yourself before God in silence and yieldedness. When your mind wanders, center yourself by returning to the spirit of the passage.

SCRIPTURE

You alone are the Lord. You made the heavens, even the heaven of heavens, and all their starry host, the earth and all that is on it, the seas and all that is in them. You give life to all that is in them, and the host of heaven worships You. (Nehemiah 9:6)

READING

Slowly read the Scripture passage several times.

MEDITATION

Take some time to reflect on the words and phrases in the text. Which words, phrases, or images speak most to you?

PRAYER

Offer the internalized passage back to God in the form of a personalized prayer of adoration, confession, renewal, petition, intercession, affirmation, or thanksgiving.

CONTEMPLATION

What word or image captures the spirit of the passage for you?

Take a few minutes to present yourself before God in silence and yieldedness. When your mind wanders, center yourself by returning to the spirit of the passage.

SCRIPTURE

God reveals deep things out of darkness and brings the shadow of death into the light. He makes nations great and destroys them; He enlarges nations and disperses them. (Job 12:22-23)

READING

Slowly read the Scripture passage several times.

MEDITATION

Take some time to reflect on the words and phrases in the text. Which words, phrases, or images speak most to you?

PRAYER

Offer the internalized passage back to God in the form of a personalized prayer of adoration, confession, renewal, petition, intercession, affirmation, or thanksgiving.

CONTEMPLATION

What word or image captures the spirit of the passage for you?

Take a few minutes to present yourself before God in silence and yieldedness. When your mind wanders, center yourself by returning to the spirit of the passage.

SCRIPTURE

God is exalted beyond our understanding; the number of His years is unsearchable. (*Job 36:26*)

READING

Slowly read the Scripture passage several times.

MEDITATION

Take some time to reflect on the words and phrases in the text. Which words, phrases, or images speak most to you?

PRAYER

Offer the internalized passage back to God in the form of a personalized prayer of adoration, confession, renewal, petition, intercession, affirmation, or thanksgiving.

CONTEMPLATION

What word or image captures the spirit of the passage for you?

Take a few minutes to present yourself before God in silence and yieldedness. When your mind wanders, center yourself by returning to the spirit of the passage.

SCRIPTURE

I know that You can do all things and that no purpose of Yours can be thwarted. (Job 42:2)

READING

Slowly read the Scripture passage several times.

MEDITATION

Take some time to reflect on the words and phrases in the text. Which words, phrases, or images speak most to you?

PRAYER

Offer the internalized passage back to God in the form of a personalized prayer of adoration, confession, renewal, petition, intercession, affirmation, or thanksgiving.

CONTEMPLATION

What word or image captures the spirit of the passage for you?

Take a few minutes to present yourself before God in silence and yieldedness. When your mind wanders, center yourself by returning to the spirit of the passage.

SCRIPTURE

From the rising of the sun to its setting, the name of the Lord is to be praised. The Lord is high above all nations, His glory above the heavens. Who is like the Lord our God, the One who is enthroned on high, who humbles Himself to behold the things that are in the heavens and in the earth? (Psalm 113:3-6)

READING

Slowly read the Scripture passage several times.

MEDITATION

Take some time to reflect on the words and phrases in the text.
Which words, phrases, or images speak most to you?

PRAYER

Offer the internalized passage back to God in the form of a personalized prayer of adoration, confession, renewal, petition, intercession, affirmation, or thanksgiving.

CONTEMPLATION

What word or image captures the spirit of the passage for you?

Take a few minutes to present yourself before God in silence and yieldedness. When your mind wanders, center yourself by returning to the spirit of the passage.

SCRIPTURE

All Your works will praise You, O Lord, and Your saints will bless You.
They will speak of the glory of Your kingdom and talk of Your power, so
that all people may know of Your mighty acts and the glorious majesty of
Your kingdom. Your kingdom is an everlasting kingdom, and Your domin-
ion endures through all generations. (Psalm 145:10-13)

READING

Slowly read the Scripture passage several times.

MEDITATION

Take some time to reflect on the words and phrases in the text.
Which words, phrases, or images speak most to you?

PRAYER

Offer the internalized passage back to God in the form of a personalized
prayer of adoration, confession, renewal, petition, intercession,
affirmation, or thanksgiving.

CONTEMPLATION

What word or image captures the spirit of the passage for you?

Take a few minutes to present yourself before God in silence and
yieldedness. When your mind wanders, center yourself by returning
to the spirit of the passage.

SCRIPTURE

Holy, Holy, Holy is the Lord of hosts; the whole earth is full of His glory.
(Isaiah 6:3)

READING

Slowly read the Scripture passage several times.

MEDITATION

Take some time to reflect on the words and phrases in the text.
Which words, phrases, or images speak most to you?

PRAYER

Offer the internalized passage back to God in the form of a personalized
prayer of adoration, confession, renewal, petition, intercession,
affirmation, or thanksgiving.

CONTEMPLATION

What word or image captures the spirit of the passage for you?

Take a few minutes to present yourself before God in silence and
yieldedness. When your mind wanders, center yourself by returning
to the spirit of the passage.

SCRIPTURE

You are the Lord, and there is no other; apart from You there is no God. From the rising to the setting of the sun, we know there is none besides You. You are the Lord, and there is no other. (Isaiah 45:5-6)

READING

Slowly read the Scripture passage several times.

MEDITATION

Take some time to reflect on the words and phrases in the text. Which words, phrases, or images speak most to you?

PRAYER

Offer the internalized passage back to God in the form of a personalized prayer of adoration, confession, renewal, petition, intercession, affirmation, or thanksgiving.

CONTEMPLATION

What word or image captures the spirit of the passage for you?

Take a few minutes to present yourself before God in silence and yieldedness. When your mind wanders, center yourself by returning to the spirit of the passage.

SCRIPTURE

You have sworn by Yourself; the word has gone out of Your mouth in righteousness and will not return. Every knee will bow before You, and every tongue will acknowledge You. (Isaiah 45:23)

READING

Slowly read the Scripture passage several times.

MEDITATION

Take some time to reflect on the words and phrases in the text. Which words, phrases, or images speak most to you?

PRAYER

Offer the internalized passage back to God in the form of a personalized prayer of adoration, confession, renewal, petition, intercession, affirmation, or thanksgiving.

CONTEMPLATION

What word or image captures the spirit of the passage for you?

Take a few minutes to present yourself before God in silence and yieldedness. When your mind wanders, center yourself by returning to the spirit of the passage.

SCRIPTURE

You declare the end from the beginning, and from ancient times things that have not yet been done, saying, "My purpose will stand, and I will do all My pleasure." (Isaiah 46:10)

READING

Slowly read the Scripture passage several times.

MEDITATION

Take some time to reflect on the words and phrases in the text. Which words, phrases, or images speak most to you?

PRAYER

Offer the internalized passage back to God in the form of a personalized prayer of adoration, confession, renewal, petition, intercession, affirmation, or thanksgiving.

CONTEMPLATION

What word or image captures the spirit of the passage for you?

Take a few minutes to present yourself before God in silence and yieldedness. When your mind wanders, center yourself by returning to the spirit of the passage.

SCRIPTURE

"My thoughts are not your thoughts, neither are your ways My ways,"
declares the Lord. "As the heavens are higher than the earth, so are My
ways higher than your ways, and My thoughts than your thoughts."
(Isaiah 55:8-9)

READING

Slowly read the Scripture passage several times.

MEDITATION

Take some time to reflect on the words and phrases in the text.
Which words, phrases, or images speak most to you?

PRAYER

Offer the internalized passage back to God in the form of a personalized
prayer of adoration, confession, renewal, petition, intercession,
affirmation, or thanksgiving.

CONTEMPLATION

What word or image captures the spirit of the passage for you?

Take a few minutes to present yourself before God in silence and
yieldedness. When your mind wanders, center yourself by returning
to the spirit of the passage.

SCRIPTURE

You are the high and lofty One who inhabits eternity, whose name is holy. You live in a high and holy place but also with him who is contrite and lowly in spirit, to revive the spirit of the lowly and to revive the heart of the contrite. (Isaiah 57:15)

READING

Slowly read the Scripture passage several times.

MEDITATION

Take some time to reflect on the words and phrases in the text. Which words, phrases, or images speak most to you?

PRAYER

Offer the internalized passage back to God in the form of a personalized prayer of adoration, confession, renewal, petition, intercession, affirmation, or thanksgiving.

CONTEMPLATION

What word or image captures the spirit of the passage for you?

Take a few minutes to present yourself before God in silence and yieldedness. When your mind wanders, center yourself by returning to the spirit of the passage.

SCRIPTURE

The Lord is the true God; He is the living God and the everlasting King. At His wrath, the earth trembles, and the nations cannot endure His indignation. (Jeremiah 10:10)

READING

Slowly read the Scripture passage several times.

MEDITATION

Take some time to reflect on the words and phrases in the text. Which words, phrases, or images speak most to you?

PRAYER

Offer the internalized passage back to God in the form of a personalized prayer of adoration, confession, renewal, petition, intercession, affirmation, or thanksgiving.

CONTEMPLATION

What word or image captures the spirit of the passage for you?

Take a few minutes to present yourself before God in silence and yieldedness. When your mind wanders, center yourself by returning to the spirit of the passage.

SCRIPTURE

Ah, Lord God! You have made the heavens and the earth by Your great power and outstretched arm. Nothing is too difficult for You. You are the great and mighty God, whose name is the Lord of hosts. You are great in counsel and mighty in deed, and Your eyes are open to all the ways of the sons of men; You reward everyone according to his ways and according to the fruit of his deeds. (Jeremiah 32:17-19)

READING

Slowly read the Scripture passage several times.

MEDITATION

Take some time to reflect on the words and phrases in the text. Which words, phrases, or images speak most to you?

PRAYER

Offer the internalized passage back to God in the form of a personalized prayer of adoration, confession, renewal, petition, intercession, affirmation, or thanksgiving.

CONTEMPLATION

What word or image captures the spirit of the passage for you?

Take a few minutes to present yourself before God in silence and yieldedness. When your mind wanders, center yourself by returning to the spirit of the passage.

SCRIPTURE

Blessed be the name of God for ever and ever, for wisdom and power belong to Him. He changes the times and the seasons; He raises up kings and deposes them. He gives wisdom to the wise and knowledge to those who have understanding. He reveals deep and hidden things; He knows what is in the darkness, and light dwells with Him. (Daniel 2:20-22)

READING

Slowly read the Scripture passage several times.

MEDITATION

Take some time to reflect on the words and phrases in the text. Which words, phrases, or images speak most to you?

PRAYER

Offer the internalized passage back to God in the form of a personalized prayer of adoration, confession, renewal, petition, intercession, affirmation, or thanksgiving.

CONTEMPLATION

What word or image captures the spirit of the passage for you?

Take a few minutes to present yourself before God in silence and yieldedness. When your mind wanders, center yourself by returning to the spirit of the passage.

SCRIPTURE

Oh, the depth of the riches both of the wisdom and knowledge of God! How unsearchable are His judgments, and His ways past finding out! For who has known the mind of the Lord? Or who has been His counselor? Or who has first given to Him, that He should repay him? For from Him and through Him and to Him are all things. To Him be the glory forever! Amen. (Romans 11:33-36)

READING

Slowly read the Scripture passage several times.

MEDITATION

Take some time to reflect on the words and phrases in the text. Which words, phrases, or images speak most to you?

PRAYER

Offer the internalized passage back to God in the form of a personalized prayer of adoration, confession, renewal, petition, intercession, affirmation, or thanksgiving.

CONTEMPLATION

What word or image captures the spirit of the passage for you?

Take a few minutes to present yourself before God in silence and yieldedness. When your mind wanders, center yourself by returning to the spirit of the passage.

SCRIPTURE

Blessed be the God and Father of our Lord Jesus Christ, the Father of mercies and the God of all comfort. (2 Corinthians 1:3)

READING

Slowly read the Scripture passage several times.

MEDITATION

Take some time to reflect on the words and phrases in the text. Which words, phrases, or images speak most to you?

PRAYER

Offer the internalized passage back to God in the form of a personalized prayer of adoration, confession, renewal, petition, intercession, affirmation, or thanksgiving.

CONTEMPLATION

What word or image captures the spirit of the passage for you?

Take a few minutes to present yourself before God in silence and yieldedness. When your mind wanders, center yourself by returning to the spirit of the passage.

SCRIPTURE

To the King eternal, immortal, invisible, the only God, be honor and glory forever and ever. (1 Timothy 1:17)

READING

Slowly read the Scripture passage several times.

MEDITATION

Take some time to reflect on the words and phrases in the text.
Which words, phrases, or images speak most to you?

PRAYER

Offer the internalized passage back to God in the form of a personalized prayer of adoration, confession, renewal, petition, intercession, affirmation, or thanksgiving.

CONTEMPLATION

What word or image captures the spirit of the passage for you?

Take a few minutes to present yourself before God in silence and yieldedness. When your mind wanders, center yourself by returning to the spirit of the passage.

SCRIPTURE

God is the blessed and only Sovereign, the King of kings and Lord of lords, who alone has immortality and dwells in unapproachable light, whom no one has seen or can see. To Him be honor and eternal dominion. (1 Timothy 6:15-16)

READING

Slowly read the Scripture passage several times.

MEDITATION

Take some time to reflect on the words and phrases in the text. Which words, phrases, or images speak most to you?

PRAYER

Offer the internalized passage back to God in the form of a personalized prayer of adoration, confession, renewal, petition, intercession, affirmation, or thanksgiving.

CONTEMPLATION

What word or image captures the spirit of the passage for you?

Take a few minutes to present yourself before God in silence and yieldedness. When your mind wanders, center yourself by returning to the spirit of the passage.

SCRIPTURE

The Lord God is the Alpha and the Omega, who is, and who was, and who is to come, the Almighty. (Revelation 1:8)

READING

Slowly read the Scripture passage several times.

MEDITATION

Take some time to reflect on the words and phrases in the text. Which words, phrases, or images speak most to you?

PRAYER

Offer the internalized passage back to God in the form of a personalized prayer of adoration, confession, renewal, petition, intercession, affirmation, or thanksgiving.

CONTEMPLATION

What word or image captures the spirit of the passage for you?

Take a few minutes to present yourself before God in silence and yieldedness. When your mind wanders, center yourself by returning to the spirit of the passage.

SCRIPTURE

To us a child is born, to us a son is given, and the government will be on His shoulders. And He will be called Wonderful Counselor, Mighty God, Everlasting Father, Prince of Peace. Of the increase of His government and peace there will be no end. He will reign on the throne of David and over his kingdom, establishing and upholding it with justice and righteousness from that time on and forever. The zeal of the Lord of hosts will accomplish this. (Isaiah 9:6-7)

READING

Slowly read the Scripture passage several times.

MEDITATION

Take some time to reflect on the words and phrases in the text. Which words, phrases, or images speak most to you?

PRAYER

Offer the internalized passage back to God in the form of a personalized prayer of adoration, confession, renewal, petition, intercession, affirmation, or thanksgiving.

CONTEMPLATION

What word or image captures the spirit of the passage for you?

Take a few minutes to present yourself before God in silence and yieldedness. When your mind wanders, center yourself by returning to the spirit of the passage.

SCRIPTURE

The Son of Man will come with the clouds of heaven. In the presence of the Ancient of Days, He will be given dominion and glory and a kingdom, so that all peoples, nations, and people of every language will worship Him. His dominion is an everlasting dominion that will not pass away, and His kingdom is one that will never be destroyed. (Daniel 7:13-14)

READING

Slowly read the Scripture passage several times.

MEDITATION

Take some time to reflect on the words and phrases in the text. Which words, phrases, or images speak most to you?

PRAYER

Offer the internalized passage back to God in the form of a personalized prayer of adoration, confession, renewal, petition, intercession, affirmation, or thanksgiving.

CONTEMPLATION

What word or image captures the spirit of the passage for you?

Take a few minutes to present yourself before God in silence and yieldedness. When your mind wanders, center yourself by returning to the spirit of the passage.

SCRIPTURE

Rejoice greatly, O daughter of Zion! Shout, O daughter of Jerusalem!
Behold, your King is coming to you; He is just and having salvation,
humble and riding on a donkey, on a colt, the foal of a donkey. He will
proclaim peace to the nations; His dominion will extend from sea to sea
and from the River to the ends of the earth. (Zechariah 9:9-10)

READING

Slowly read the Scripture passage several times.

MEDITATION

Take some time to reflect on the words and phrases in the text.
Which words, phrases, or images speak most to you?

PRAYER

Offer the internalized passage back to God in the form of a personalized
prayer of adoration, confession, renewal, petition, intercession,
affirmation, or thanksgiving.

CONTEMPLATION

What word or image captures the spirit of the passage for you?

Take a few minutes to present yourself before God in silence and
yieldedness. When your mind wanders, center yourself by returning
to the spirit of the passage.

SCRIPTURE

Jesus rejoiced in the Holy Spirit, and said, "I praise You, Father, Lord of heaven and earth, because You have hidden these things from the wise and learned, and revealed them to little children. Yes, Father, for this was well-pleasing in Your sight. All things have been delivered to Me by My Father. No one knows the Son except the Father, and no one knows the Father except the Son and those to whom the Son chooses to reveal Him."
(Matthew 11:25-27; Luke 10:21-22)

READING

Slowly read the Scripture passage several times.

MEDITATION

Take some time to reflect on the words and phrases in the text.
Which words, phrases, or images speak most to you?

PRAYER

Offer the internalized passage back to God in the form of a personalized prayer of adoration, confession, renewal, petition, intercession, affirmation, or thanksgiving.

CONTEMPLATION

What word or image captures the spirit of the passage for you?

Take a few minutes to present yourself before God in silence and yieldedness. When your mind wanders, center yourself by returning to the spirit of the passage.

SCRIPTURE

Lord, You have said, "Come to Me, all you who labor and are heavy laden, and I will give you rest. Take My yoke upon you and learn from Me, for I am gentle and humble in heart, and you will find rest for your souls. For My yoke is easy, and My burden is light." (Matthew 11:28-30)

READING

Slowly read the Scripture passage several times.

MEDITATION

Take some time to reflect on the words and phrases in the text. Which words, phrases, or images speak most to you?

PRAYER

Offer the internalized passage back to God in the form of a personalized prayer of adoration, confession, renewal, petition, intercession, affirmation, or thanksgiving.

CONTEMPLATION

What word or image captures the spirit of the passage for you?

Take a few minutes to present yourself before God in silence and yieldedness. When your mind wanders, center yourself by returning to the spirit of the passage.

SCRIPTURE

The Son of Man did not come to be served, but to serve, and to give His life as a ransom for many. (Matthew 20:28)

READING

Slowly read the Scripture passage several times.

MEDITATION

Take some time to reflect on the words and phrases in the text.
Which words, phrases, or images speak most to you?

PRAYER

Offer the internalized passage back to God in the form of a personalized prayer of adoration, confession, renewal, petition, intercession, affirmation, or thanksgiving.

CONTEMPLATION

What word or image captures the spirit of the passage for you?

Take a few minutes to present yourself before God in silence and yieldedness. When your mind wanders, center yourself by returning to the spirit of the passage.

SCRIPTURE

When the Son of Man comes in His glory, and all the angels with Him, He
will sit on His glorious throne. All the nations will be gathered before
Him, and He will separate the people one from another as a shepherd sep-
arates the sheep from the goats. He will put the sheep on His right and the
goats on His left. Then the King will say to those on His right, "Come,
you who are blessed by My Father; inherit the kingdom prepared for you
since the foundation of the world." (Matthew 25:31-34)

READING

Slowly read the Scripture passage several times.

MEDITATION

Take some time to reflect on the words and phrases in the text.
Which words, phrases, or images speak most to you?

PRAYER

Offer the internalized passage back to God in the form of a personalized
prayer of adoration, confession, renewal, petition, intercession,
affirmation, or thanksgiving.

CONTEMPLATION

What word or image captures the spirit of the passage for you?

Take a few minutes to present yourself before God in silence and
yieldedness. When your mind wanders, center yourself by returning
to the spirit of the passage.

SCRIPTURE

In the beginning was the Word, and the Word was with God, and the Word was God. He was in the beginning with God. Through Him all things were made, and without Him nothing was made that has been made. In Him was life, and the life was the light of men. (John 1:1-4)

READING

Slowly read the Scripture passage several times.

MEDITATION

Take some time to reflect on the words and phrases in the text. Which words, phrases, or images speak most to you?

PRAYER

Offer the internalized passage back to God in the form of a personalized prayer of adoration, confession, renewal, petition, intercession, affirmation, or thanksgiving.

CONTEMPLATION

What word or image captures the spirit of the passage for you?

Take a few minutes to present yourself before God in silence and yieldedness. When your mind wanders, center yourself by returning to the spirit of the passage.

SCRIPTURE

The Word became flesh and dwelt among us. We have seen His glory, the glory of the only begotten of the Father, full of grace and truth. From His fullness we have all received, and grace upon grace. For the law was given through Moses; grace and truth came through Jesus Christ. No one has ever seen God, but the only begotten God, who is in the bosom of the Father, has made Him known. (John 1:14,16-18)

READING

Slowly read the Scripture passage several times.

MEDITATION

Take some time to reflect on the words and phrases in the text. Which words, phrases, or images speak most to you?

PRAYER

Offer the internalized passage back to God in the form of a personalized prayer of adoration, confession, renewal, petition, intercession, affirmation, or thanksgiving.

CONTEMPLATION

What word or image captures the spirit of the passage for you?

Take a few minutes to present yourself before God in silence and yieldedness. When your mind wanders, center yourself by returning to the spirit of the passage.

SCRIPTURE

God so loved the world that He gave His only begotten Son, that whoever believes in Him should not perish but have eternal life. For God did not send His Son into the world to condemn the world, but to save the world through Him. (John 3:16-17)

READING

Slowly read the Scripture passage several times.

MEDITATION

Take some time to reflect on the words and phrases in the text. Which words, phrases, or images speak most to you?

PRAYER

Offer the internalized passage back to God in the form of a personalized prayer of adoration, confession, renewal, petition, intercession, affirmation, or thanksgiving.

CONTEMPLATION

What word or image captures the spirit of the passage for you?

Take a few minutes to present yourself before God in silence and yieldedness. When your mind wanders, center yourself by returning to the spirit of the passage.

SCRIPTURE

The Father judges no one, but has given all judgment to the Son, that all may honor the Son just as they honor the Father. He who does not honor the Son does not honor the Father who sent Him. (John 5:22-23)

READING

Slowly read the Scripture passage several times.

MEDITATION

Take some time to reflect on the words and phrases in the text.
Which words, phrases, or images speak most to you?

PRAYER

Offer the internalized passage back to God in the form of a personalized prayer of adoration, confession, renewal, petition, intercession, affirmation, or thanksgiving.

CONTEMPLATION

What word or image captures the spirit of the passage for you?

Take a few minutes to present yourself before God in silence and yieldedness. When your mind wanders, center yourself by returning to the spirit of the passage.

SCRIPTURE

Jesus said to Martha, "I am the resurrection and the life. He who believes in Me will live, even though he dies, and whoever lives and believes in Me will never die." (John 11:25-26)

READING

Slowly read the Scripture passage several times.

MEDITATION

Take some time to reflect on the words and phrases in the text.
Which words, phrases, or images speak most to you?

PRAYER

Offer the internalized passage back to God in the form of a personalized prayer of adoration, confession, renewal, petition, intercession, affirmation, or thanksgiving.

CONTEMPLATION

What word or image captures the spirit of the passage for you?

Take a few minutes to present yourself before God in silence and yieldedness. When your mind wanders, center yourself by returning to the spirit of the passage.

SCRIPTURE

There is but one God, the Father, from whom all things came and for whom I live; and there is but one Lord, Jesus Christ, through whom all things came and through whom I live. (1 Corinthians 8:6)

READING

Slowly read the Scripture passage several times.

MEDITATION

Take some time to reflect on the words and phrases in the text. Which words, phrases, or images speak most to you?

PRAYER

Offer the internalized passage back to God in the form of a personalized prayer of adoration, confession, renewal, petition, intercession, affirmation, or thanksgiving.

CONTEMPLATION

What word or image captures the spirit of the passage for you?

Take a few minutes to present yourself before God in silence and yieldedness. When your mind wanders, center yourself by returning to the spirit of the passage.

SCRIPTURE

God highly exalted Christ Jesus and gave Him the name that is above every name, that at the name of Jesus every knee should bow, in heaven and on earth and under the earth, and every tongue should confess that Jesus Christ is Lord, to the glory of God the Father. (Philippians 2:9-11)

READING

Slowly read the Scripture passage several times.

MEDITATION

Take some time to reflect on the words and phrases in the text. Which words, phrases, or images speak most to you?

PRAYER

Offer the internalized passage back to God in the form of a personalized prayer of adoration, confession, renewal, petition, intercession, affirmation, or thanksgiving.

CONTEMPLATION

What word or image captures the spirit of the passage for you?

Take a few minutes to present yourself before God in silence and yieldedness. When your mind wanders, center yourself by returning to the spirit of the passage.

SCRIPTURE

Christ is the image of the invisible God, the firstborn over all creation. For by Him all things were created that are in heaven and on earth, visible and invisible, whether thrones or dominions or rulers or authorities; all things were created by Him and for Him. And He is before all things, and in Him all things hold together. (Colossians 1:15-17)

READING

Slowly read the Scripture passage several times.

MEDITATION

Take some time to reflect on the words and phrases in the text. Which words, phrases, or images speak most to you?

PRAYER

Offer the internalized passage back to God in the form of a personalized prayer of adoration, confession, renewal, petition, intercession, affirmation, or thanksgiving.

CONTEMPLATION

What word or image captures the spirit of the passage for you?

Take a few minutes to present yourself before God in silence and yieldedness. When your mind wanders, center yourself by returning to the spirit of the passage.

SCRIPTURE

In Christ are hidden all the treasures of wisdom and knowledge. In Him all the fullness of the Godhead lives in bodily form. (Colossians 2:3,9)

READING

Slowly read the Scripture passage several times.

MEDITATION

Take some time to reflect on the words and phrases in the text. Which words, phrases, or images speak most to you?

PRAYER

Offer the internalized passage back to God in the form of a personalized prayer of adoration, confession, renewal, petition, intercession, affirmation, or thanksgiving.

CONTEMPLATION

What word or image captures the spirit of the passage for you?

Take a few minutes to present yourself before God in silence and yieldedness. When your mind wanders, center yourself by returning to the spirit of the passage.

SCRIPTURE

We are looking for the blessed hope and the glorious appearing of our great God and Savior, Christ Jesus, who gave Himself for us to redeem us from all iniquity and to purify for Himself a people for His own possession, zealous for good works. (Titus 2:13-14)

READING

Slowly read the Scripture passage several times.

MEDITATION

Take some time to reflect on the words and phrases in the text. Which words, phrases, or images speak most to you?

PRAYER

Offer the internalized passage back to God in the form of a personalized prayer of adoration, confession, renewal, petition, intercession, affirmation, or thanksgiving.

CONTEMPLATION

What word or image captures the spirit of the passage for you?

Take a few minutes to present yourself before God in silence and yieldedness. When your mind wanders, center yourself by returning to the spirit of the passage.

SCRIPTURE

In the past God spoke to the fathers through the prophets at many times and in various ways, but in these last days He has spoken to us by His Son, whom He appointed heir of all things, and through whom He made the universe. (Hebrews 1:1-2)

READING

Slowly read the Scripture passage several times.

MEDITATION

Take some time to reflect on the words and phrases in the text. Which words, phrases, or images speak most to you?

PRAYER

Offer the internalized passage back to God in the form of a personalized prayer of adoration, confession, renewal, petition, intercession, affirmation, or thanksgiving.

CONTEMPLATION

What word or image captures the spirit of the passage for you?

Take a few minutes to present yourself before God in silence and yieldedness. When your mind wanders, center yourself by returning to the spirit of the passage.

SCRIPTURE

The Son is the radiance of God's glory and the exact representation of His being, upholding all things by His powerful word. After He cleansed our sins, He sat down at the right hand of the Majesty on high, having become as much superior to angels as the name He has inherited is more excellent than theirs. (Hebrews 1:3-4)

READING

Slowly read the Scripture passage several times.

MEDITATION

Take some time to reflect on the words and phrases in the text. Which words, phrases, or images speak most to you?

PRAYER

Offer the internalized passage back to God in the form of a personalized prayer of adoration, confession, renewal, petition, intercession, affirmation, or thanksgiving.

CONTEMPLATION

What word or image captures the spirit of the passage for you?

Take a few minutes to present yourself before God in silence and yieldedness. When your mind wanders, center yourself by returning to the spirit of the passage.

SCRIPTURE

We see Jesus, who was made a little lower than the angels, now crowned with glory and honor because He suffered death, that by the grace of God He might taste death for everyone. For it was fitting for Him, for whom are all things and through whom are all things, in bringing many sons to glory, to make the author of their salvation perfect through sufferings. (Hebrews 2:9-10)

READING

Slowly read the Scripture passage several times.

MEDITATION

Tak some time to reflect on the words and phrases in the text.
Which words, phrases, or images speak most to you?

PRAYER

Offer the internalized passage back to God in the form of a personalized prayer of adoration, confession, renewal, petition, intercession, affirmation, or thanksgiving.

CONTEMPLATION

What word or image captures the spirit of the passage for you?

Take a few minutes to present yourself before God in silence and yieldedness. When your mind wanders, center yourself by returning to the spirit of the passage.

SCRIPTURE

Christ had to be made like His brothers in every way, in order that He might become a merciful and faithful high priest in things pertaining to God, to make propitiation for the sins of the people. Because He Himself suffered when He was tempted, He is able to help those who are being tempted. (Hebrews 2:17-18)

READING

Slowly read the Scripture passage several times.

MEDITATION

Take some time to reflect on the words and phrases in the text. Which words, phrases, or images speak most to you?

PRAYER

Offer the internalized passage back to God in the form of a personalized prayer of adoration, confession, renewal, petition, intercession, affirmation, or thanksgiving.

CONTEMPLATION

What word or image captures the spirit of the passage for you?

Take a few minutes to present yourself before God in silence and yieldedness. When your mind wanders, center yourself by returning to the spirit of the passage.

SCRIPTURE

The Word of God is living and active and sharper than any double-edged sword, piercing even to the dividing of soul and spirit and of joints and marrow, and it judges the thoughts and attitudes of the heart. And there is no creature hidden from His sight, but everything is uncovered and laid bare before the eyes of Him to whom we must give account.
(Hebrews 4:12-13)

READING

Slowly read the Scripture passage several times.

MEDITATION

Take some time to reflect on the words and phrases in the text.
Which words, phrases, or images speak most to you?

PRAYER

Offer the internalized passage back to God in the form of a personalized prayer of adoration, confession, renewal, petition, intercession, affirmation, or thanksgiving.

CONTEMPLATION

What word or image captures the spirit of the passage for you?

Take a few minutes to present yourself before God in silence and yieldedness. When your mind wanders, center yourself by returning to the spirit of the passage.

SCRIPTURE
Jesus Christ is the same yesterday, today, and forever. (Hebrews 13:8)

READING
Slowly read the Scripture passage several times.

MEDITATION
Take some time to reflect on the words and phrases in the text.
Which words, phrases, or images speak most to you?

PRAYER
Offer the internalized passage back to God in the form of a personalized
prayer of adoration, confession, renewal, petition, intercession,
affirmation, or thanksgiving.

CONTEMPLATION
What word or image captures the spirit of the passage for you?

Take a few minutes to present yourself before God in silence and
yieldedness. When your mind wanders, center yourself by returning
to the spirit of the passage.

SCRIPTURE

The Lord Jesus Christ received honor and glory from God the Father when the voice came to Him from the Majestic Glory who said, "This is My beloved Son, with whom I am well pleased." (2 Peter 1:17)

READING

Slowly read the Scripture passage several times.

MEDITATION

Take some time to reflect on the words and phrases in the text. Which words, phrases, or images speak most to you?

PRAYER

Offer the internalized passage back to God in the form of a personalized prayer of adoration, confession, renewal, petition, intercession, affirmation, or thanksgiving.

CONTEMPLATION

What word or image captures the spirit of the passage for you?

Take a few minutes to present yourself before God in silence and yieldedness. When your mind wanders, center yourself by returning to the spirit of the passage.

SCRIPTURE

By this the love of God was manifested to us, that God has sent His only begotten Son into the world that we might live through Him. In this is love, not that we loved God, but that He loved us and sent His Son to be the propitiation for our sins. (1 John 4:9-10)

READING

Slowly read the Scripture passage several times.

MEDITATION

Take some time to reflect on the words and phrases in the text. Which words, phrases, or images speak most to you?

PRAYER

Offer the internalized passage back to God in the form of a personalized prayer of adoration, confession, renewal, petition, intercession, affirmation, or thanksgiving.

CONTEMPLATION

What word or image captures the spirit of the passage for you?

Take a few minutes to present yourself before God in silence and yieldedness. When your mind wanders, center yourself by returning to the spirit of the passage.

SCRIPTURE

Jesus Christ is the faithful witness, the firstborn from the dead, and the ruler of the kings of the earth. To Him who loves us and has freed us from our sins by His blood and has made us to be a kingdom and priests to serve His God and Father; to Him be glory and power for ever and ever. (Revelation 1:5-6)

READING

Slowly read the Scripture passage several times.

MEDITATION

Take some time to reflect on the words and phrases in the text. Which words, phrases, or images speak most to you?

PRAYER

Offer the internalized passage back to God in the form of a personalized prayer of adoration, confession, renewal, petition, intercession, affirmation, or thanksgiving.

CONTEMPLATION

What word or image captures the spirit of the passage for you?

Take a few minutes to present yourself before God in silence and yieldedness. When your mind wanders, center yourself by returning to the spirit of the passage.

SCRIPTURE

The Lord Jesus is the First and the Last, and the Living One; He was dead,
and behold He is alive forevermore and holds the keys of death and of
Hades. (Revelation 1:17-18)

READING

Slowly read the Scripture passage several times.

MEDITATION

Take some time to reflect on the words and phrases in the text.
Which words, phrases, or images speak most to you?

PRAYER

Offer the internalized passage back to God in the form of a personalized
prayer of adoration, confession, renewal, petition, intercession,
affirmation, or thanksgiving.

CONTEMPLATION

What word or image captures the spirit of the passage for you?

Take a few minutes to present yourself before God in silence and
yieldedness. When your mind wanders, center yourself by returning
to the spirit of the passage.

SCRIPTURE

The Lord Jesus, who is holy and true, holds the key of David. What He opens no one can shut, and what He shuts no one can open.
(Revelation 3:7)

READING

Slowly read the Scripture passage several times.

MEDITATION

Take some time to reflect on the words and phrases in the text. Which words, phrases, or images speak most to you?

PRAYER

Offer the internalized passage back to God in the form of a personalized prayer of adoration, confession, renewal, petition, intercession, affirmation, or thanksgiving.

CONTEMPLATION

What word or image captures the spirit of the passage for you?

Take a few minutes to present yourself before God in silence and yieldedness. When your mind wanders, center yourself by returning to the spirit of the passage.

SCRIPTURE

John looked and heard the voice of many angels encircling the throne and the living creatures and the elders; and their number was myriads of myriads, and thousands of thousands, saying with a loud voice, "Worthy is the Lamb, who was slain, to receive power and riches and wisdom and strength and honor and glory and blessing!" (Revelation 5:11-12)

READING

Slowly read the Scripture passage several times.

MEDITATION

Take some time to reflect on the words and phrases in the text. Which words, phrases, or images speak most to you?

PRAYER

Offer the internalized passage back to God in the form of a personalized prayer of adoration, confession, renewal, petition, intercession, affirmation, or thanksgiving.

CONTEMPLATION

What word or image captures the spirit of the passage for you?

Take a few minutes to present yourself before God in silence and yieldedness. When your mind wanders, center yourself by returning to the spirit of the passage.

SCRIPTURE

The Lord Jesus is coming quickly. His reward is with Him, and He will give to everyone according to what he has done. He is the Alpha and the Omega, the First and the Last, the Beginning and the End. Yes, He is coming quickly. Amen. Come, Lord Jesus. (Revelation 22:12-13,20)

READING

Slowly read the Scripture passage several times.

MEDITATION

Take some time to reflect on the words and phrases in the text. Which words, phrases, or images speak most to you?

PRAYER

Offer the internalized passage back to God in the form of a personalized prayer of adoration, confession, renewal, petition, intercession, affirmation, or thanksgiving.

CONTEMPLATION

What word or image captures the spirit of the passage for you?

Take a few minutes to present yourself before God in silence and yieldedness. When your mind wanders, center yourself by returning to the spirit of the passage.

SCRIPTURE

Where can I go from Your Spirit? Or where can I flee from Your presence? If I ascend to heaven, You are there; if I make my bed in Sheol, You are there. If I take the wings of the dawn, if I dwell in the furthest part of the sea, even there Your hand will lead me; Your right hand will lay hold of me. If I say, "Surely the darkness will cover me," even the night will be light around me. The darkness is not dark to You, and the night shines as the day; darkness and light are alike to You. (Psalm 139:7-12)

READING

Slowly read the Scripture passage several times.

MEDITATION

Take some time to reflect on the words and phrases in the text.
Which words, phrases, or images speak most to you?

PRAYER

Offer the internalized passage back to God in the form of a personalized prayer of adoration, confession, renewal, petition, intercession, affirmation, or thanksgiving.

CONTEMPLATION

What word or image captures the spirit of the passage for you?

Take a few minutes to present yourself before God in silence and yieldedness. When your mind wanders, center yourself by returning to the spirit of the passage.

SCRIPTURE

A Shoot will come forth from the stump of Jesse; from his roots a Branch will bear fruit. The Spirit of the Lord will rest on Him—the Spirit of wisdom and of understanding, the Spirit of counsel and of power, the Spirit of knowledge and of the fear of the Lord—and He will delight in the fear of the Lord. He will not judge by what He sees with His eyes, or decide by what He hears with His ears, but with righteousness He will judge the poor and decide with fairness for the meek of the earth. And He will strike the earth with the rod of His mouth; with the breath of His lips He will slay the wicked. Righteousness will be His belt, and faithfulness the sash around His waist. (Isaiah 11:1-5)

READING

Slowly read the Scripture passage several times.

MEDITATION

Take some time to reflect on the words and phrases in the text. Which words, phrases, or images speak most to you?

PRAYER

Offer the internalized passage back to God in the form of a personalized prayer of adoration, confession, renewal, petition, intercession, affirmation, or thanksgiving.

CONTEMPLATION

What word or image captures the spirit of the passage for you?

Take a few minutes to present yourself before God in silence and yieldedness. When your mind wanders, center yourself by returning to the spirit of the passage.

SCRIPTURE

Jesus fulfilled the words of the prophet Isaiah: "The Spirit of the Lord is upon me, because He has anointed me to preach good news to the poor. He has sent me to proclaim freedom for the captives and recovery of sight to the blind, to set free those who are downtrodden, to proclaim the acceptable year of the Lord." (Luke 4:18-19)

READING

Slowly read the Scripture passage several times.

MEDITATION

Take some time to reflect on the words and phrases in the text. Which words, phrases, or images speak most to you?

PRAYER

Offer the internalized passage back to God in the form of a personalized prayer of adoration, confession, renewal, petition, intercession, affirmation, or thanksgiving.

CONTEMPLATION

What word or image captures the spirit of the passage for you?

Take a few minutes to present yourself before God in silence and yieldedness. When your mind wanders, center yourself by returning to the spirit of the passage.

SCRIPTURE

Unless one is born again, he cannot see the kingdom of God; unless one is born of water and the Spirit, he cannot enter into the kingdom of God. That which is born of the flesh is flesh, and that which is born of the Spirit is spirit. The wind blows wherever it pleases, and we hear its sound, but we cannot tell where it comes from, or where it is going. So it is with everyone born of the Spirit. (John 3:3,5-6,8)

READING

Slowly read the Scripture passage several times.

MEDITATION

Take some time to reflect on the words and phrases in the text. Which words, phrases, or images speak most to you?

PRAYER

Offer the internalized passage back to God in the form of a personalized prayer of adoration, confession, renewal, petition, intercession, affirmation, or thanksgiving.

CONTEMPLATION

What word or image captures the spirit of the passage for you?

Take a few minutes to present yourself before God in silence and yieldedness. When your mind wanders, center yourself by returning to the spirit of the passage.

SCRIPTURE

He who comes from above is above all; he who is from the earth belongs to the earth, and speaks as one from the earth. He who comes from heaven is above all. He whom God has sent speaks the words of God, for He gives the Spirit without limit. (John 3:31,34)

READING

Slowly read the Scripture passage several times.

MEDITATION

Which words, phrases, or images speak most to you?

PRAYER

Offer the internalized passage back to God in the form of a personalized prayer of adoration, confession, renewal, petition, intercession, affirmation, or thanksgiving.

CONTEMPLATION

What word or image captures the spirit of the passage for you?

Take a few minutes to present yourself before God in silence and yieldedness. When your mind wanders, center yourself by returning to the spirit of the passage.

SCRIPTURE

You have asked the Father, and He has given me another Comforter to be with me forever, even the Spirit of truth, whom the world cannot receive, because it neither sees Him nor knows Him. But I know Him, for He lives in me. (John 14:16-17)

READING

Slowly read the Scripture passage several times.

MEDITATION

Take some time to reflect on the words and phrases in the text.
Which words, phrases, or images speak most to you?

PRAYER

Offer the internalized passage back to God in the form of a personalized prayer of adoration, confession, renewal, petition, intercession, affirmation, or thanksgiving.

CONTEMPLATION

What word or image captures the spirit of the passage for you?

Take a few minutes to present yourself before God in silence and yieldedness. When your mind wanders, center yourself by returning to the spirit of the passage.

SCRIPTURE

But I tell you the truth: It is to your advantage that I am going away. For if I do not go away, the Advocate will not come to you; but if I go, I will send Him to you. (John 16:7)

READING

Slowly read the Scripture passage several times.

MEDITATION

Take some time to reflect on the words and phrases in the text. Which words, phrases, or images speak most to you?

PRAYER

Offer the internalized passage back to God in the form of a personalized prayer of adoration, confession, renewal, petition, intercession, affirmation, or thanksgiving.

CONTEMPLATION

What word or image captures the spirit of the passage for you?

Take a few minutes to present yourself before God in silence and yieldedness. When your mind wanders, center yourself by returning to the spirit of the passage.

SCRIPTURE

Jesus told His disciples, "The Spirit will glorify Me by taking from what is Mine and making it known to you. All that belongs to the Father is Mine. Therefore I said that He will take from what is Mine and make it known to you." (John 16:14-15)

READING

Slowly read the Scripture passage several times.

MEDITATION

Take some time to reflect on the words and phrases in the text. Which words, phrases, or images speak most to you?

PRAYER

Offer the internalized passage back to God in the form of a personalized prayer of adoration, confession, renewal, petition, intercession, affirmation, or thanksgiving.

CONTEMPLATION

What word or image captures the spirit of the passage for you?

Take a few minutes to present yourself before God in silence and yieldedness. When your mind wanders, center yourself by returning to the spirit of the passage.

SCRIPTURE

The Lord told the apostles, "You will receive power when the Holy Spirit comes upon you; and you will be My witnesses in Jerusalem, and in all Judea and Samaria, and to the ends of the earth." (Acts 1:8)

READING

Slowly read the Scripture passage several times.

MEDITATION

Take some time to reflect on the words and phrases in the text. Which words, phrases, or images speak most to you?

PRAYER

Offer the internalized passage back to God in the form of a personalized prayer of adoration, confession, renewal, petition, intercession, affirmation, or thanksgiving.

CONTEMPLATION

What word or image captures the spirit of the passage for you?

Take a few minutes to present yourself before God in silence and yieldedness. When your mind wanders, center yourself by returning to the spirit of the passage.

SCRIPTURE

There is now no condemnation for those who are in Christ Jesus, because the law of the Spirit of life in Christ Jesus has set me free from the law of sin and death. (Romans 8:1-2)

READING

Slowly read the Scripture passage several times.

MEDITATION

Take some time to reflect on the words and phrases in the text. Which words, phrases, or images speak most to you?

PRAYER

Offer the internalized passage back to God in the form of a personalized prayer of adoration, confession, renewal, petition, intercession, affirmation, or thanksgiving.

CONTEMPLATION

What word or image captures the spirit of the passage for you?

Take a few minutes to present yourself before God in silence and yieldedness. When your mind wanders, center yourself by returning to the spirit of the passage.

SCRIPTURE

Those who live according to the flesh set their minds on the things of the flesh; but those who live according to the Spirit set their minds on the things of the Spirit. The mind of the flesh is death, but the mind of the Spirit is life and peace. (Romans 8:5-6)

READING

Slowly read the Scripture passage several times.

MEDITATION

Take some time to reflect on the words and phrases in the text. Which words, phrases, or images speak most to you?

PRAYER

Offer the internalized passage back to God in the form of a personalized prayer of adoration, confession, renewal, petition, intercession, affirmation, or thanksgiving.

CONTEMPLATION

What word or image captures the spirit of the passage for you?

Take a few minutes to present yourself before God in silence and yieldedness. When your mind wanders, center yourself by returning to the spirit of the passage.

SCRIPTURE

*I am not in the flesh but in the Spirit, since the Spirit of God lives in me.
And if anyone does not have the Spirit of Christ, he does not belong to
Him. If Christ is in me, my body is dead because of sin, yet my spirit is
alive because of righteousness. And if the Spirit of Him who raised Jesus
from the dead is living in me, He who raised Christ from the dead will
also give life to my mortal body through His Spirit, who lives in me.
(Romans 8:9-11)*

READING

Slowly read the Scripture passage several times.

MEDITATION

Take some time to reflect on the words and phrases in the text.
Which words, phrases, or images speak most to you?

PRAYER

Offer the internalized passage back to God in the form of a personalized
prayer of adoration, confession, renewal, petition, intercession,
affirmation, or thanksgiving.

CONTEMPLATION

What word or image captures the spirit of the passage for you?

Take a few minutes to present yourself before God in silence and
yieldedness. When your mind wanders, center yourself by returning
to the spirit of the passage.

SCRIPTURE

If I live according to the flesh, I will die; but if by the Spirit I put to death the deeds of the body, I will live. For those who are led by the Spirit of God are sons of God. I did not receive a spirit of slavery again to fear, but I received the Spirit of adoption by whom I cry, "Abba, Father." The Spirit Himself testifies with my spirit that I am a child of God. (Romans 8:13-16)

READING

Slowly read the Scripture passage several times.

MEDITATION

Take some time to reflect on the words and phrases in the text.
Which words, phrases, or images speak most to you?

PRAYER

Offer the internalized passage back to God in the form of a personalized prayer of adoration, confession, renewal, petition, intercession, affirmation, or thanksgiving.

CONTEMPLATION

What word or image captures the spirit of the passage for you?

Take a few minutes to present yourself before God in silence and yieldedness. When your mind wanders, center yourself by returning to the spirit of the passage.

SCRIPTURE

The Spirit helps me in my weakness, for I do not know what I ought to pray for, but the Spirit Himself intercedes for me with groans that words cannot express. And He who searches the hearts knows the mind of the Spirit, because the Spirit intercedes for the saints according to the will of God. (Romans 8:26-27)

READING

Slowly read the Scripture passage several times.

MEDITATION

Take some time to reflect on the words and phrases in the text. Which words, phrases, or images speak most to you?

PRAYER

Offer the internalized passage back to God in the form of a personalized prayer of adoration, confession, renewal, petition, intercession, affirmation, or thanksgiving.

CONTEMPLATION

What word or image captures the spirit of the passage for you?

Take a few minutes to present yourself before God in silence and yieldedness. When your mind wanders, center yourself by returning to the spirit of the passage.

SCRIPTURE

The kingdom of God is not a matter of eating and drinking, but of right-eousness and peace and joy in the Holy Spirit. (Romans 14:17)

READING

Slowly read the Scripture passage several times.

MEDITATION

Take some time to reflect on the words and phrases in the text.
Which words, phrases, or images speak most to you?

PRAYER

Offer the internalized passage back to God in the form of a personalized
prayer of adoration, confession, renewal, petition, intercession,
affirmation, or thanksgiving.

CONTEMPLATION

What word or image captures the spirit of the passage for you?

Take a few minutes to present yourself before God in silence and
yieldedness. When your mind wanders, center yourself by returning
to the spirit of the passage.

SCRIPTURE

I was washed, I was sanctified, I was justified in the name of the Lord Jesus Christ and by the Spirit of our God. (1 Corinthians 6:11)

READING

Slowly read the Scripture passage several times.

MEDITATION

Take some time to reflect on the words and phrases in the text. Which words, phrases, or images speak most to you?

PRAYER

Offer the internalized passage back to God in the form of a personalized prayer of adoration, confession, renewal, petition, intercession, affirmation, or thanksgiving.

CONTEMPLATION

What word or image captures the spirit of the passage for you?

Take a few minutes to present yourself before God in silence and yieldedness. When your mind wanders, center yourself by returning to the spirit of the passage.

SCRIPTURE

There are different kinds of gifts, but the same Spirit. And there are different kinds of service, but the same Lord. And there are different kinds of working, but the same God works all of them in all people. But to each one the manifestation of the Spirit is given for the common good. (1 Corinthians 12:4-7)

READING

Slowly read the Scripture passage several times.

MEDITATION

Take some time to reflect on the words and phrases in the text. Which words, phrases, or images speak most to you?

PRAYER

Offer the internalized passage back to God in the form of a personalized prayer of adoration, confession, renewal, petition, intercession, affirmation, or thanksgiving.

CONTEMPLATION

What word or image captures the spirit of the passage for you?

Take a few minutes to present yourself before God in silence and yieldedness. When your mind wanders, center yourself by returning to the spirit of the passage.

SCRIPTURE

We were all baptized by one Spirit into one body—whether Jews or Greeks, slave or free—and we were all given the one Spirit to drink. (*1 Corinthians 12:13*)

READING

Slowly read the Scripture passage several times.

MEDITATION

Take some time to reflect on the words and phrases in the text. Which words, phrases, or images speak most to you?

PRAYER

Offer the internalized passage back to God in the form of a personalized prayer of adoration, confession, renewal, petition, intercession, affirmation, or thanksgiving.

CONTEMPLATION

What word or image captures the spirit of the passage for you?

Take a few minutes to present yourself before God in silence and yieldedness. When your mind wanders, center yourself by returning to the spirit of the passage.

SCRIPTURE

We are an epistle from Christ, written not with ink, but with the Spirit of the living God, not on tablets of stone, but on tablets of human hearts. (2 Corinthians 3:3)

READING

Slowly read the Scripture passage several times.

MEDITATION

Take some time to reflect on the words and phrases in the text. Which words, phrases, or images speak most to you?

PRAYER

Offer the internalized passage back to God in the form of a personalized prayer of adoration, confession, renewal, petition, intercession, affirmation, or thanksgiving.

CONTEMPLATION

What word or image captures the spirit of the passage for you?

Take a few minutes to present yourself before God in silence and yieldedness. When your mind wanders, center yourself by returning to the spirit of the passage.

SCRIPTURE

The Lord is the Spirit, and where the Spirit of the Lord is, there is freedom. But we all, with unveiled face beholding as in a mirror the glory of the Lord, are being transformed into the same image from glory to glory, which comes from the Lord, who is the Spirit. (2 Corinthians 3:17-18)

READING

Slowly read the Scripture passage several times.

MEDITATION

Take some time to reflect on the words and phrases in the text.
Which words, phrases, or images speak most to you?

PRAYER

Offer the internalized passage back to God in the form of a personalized prayer of adoration, confession, renewal, petition, intercession, affirmation, or thanksgiving.

CONTEMPLATION

What word or image captures the spirit of the passage for you?

Take a few minutes to present yourself before God in silence and yieldedness. When your mind wanders, center yourself by returning to the spirit of the passage.

SCRIPTURE

The grace of the Lord Jesus Christ and the love of God and the fellowship of the Holy Spirit are with me. (2 Corinthians 13:14)

READING

Slowly read the Scripture passage several times.

MEDITATION

Take some time to reflect on the words and phrases in the text. Which words, phrases, or images speak most to you?

PRAYER

Offer the internalized passage back to God in the form of a personalized prayer of adoration, confession, renewal, petition, intercession, affirmation, or thanksgiving.

CONTEMPLATION

What word or image captures the spirit of the passage for you?

Take a few minutes to present yourself before God in silence and yieldedness. When your mind wanders, center yourself by returning to the spirit of the passage.

SCRIPTURE

As I walk in the Spirit, I will not fulfill the desires of the flesh. For the flesh desires what is contrary to the Spirit, and the Spirit what is contrary to the flesh; for they oppose each other, so that I may not do the things that I wish. But if I am led by the Spirit, I am not under the law. (Galatians 5:16-18)

READING

Slowly read the Scripture passage several times.

MEDITATION

Take some time to reflect on the words and phrases in the text. Which words, phrases, or images speak most to you?

PRAYER

Offer the internalized passage back to God in the form of a personalized prayer of adoration, confession, renewal, petition, intercession, affirmation, or thanksgiving.

CONTEMPLATION

What word or image captures the spirit of the passage for you?

Take a few minutes to present yourself before God in silence and yieldedness. When your mind wanders, center yourself by returning to the spirit of the passage.

SCRIPTURE

The works of the flesh are evident, which are: immorality, impurity, sensuality, idolatry, sorcery, hatred, discord, jealousy, fits of rage, selfish ambition, dissensions, factions, envyings, drunkenness, revelries, and the like. Those who practice such things will not inherit the kingdom of God. But the fruit of the Spirit is love, joy, peace, patience, kindness, goodness, faithfulness, gentleness, self-control; against such things there is no law. Since I live in the Spirit, I will also walk in the Spirit. (Galatians 5:19-23,25)

READING

Slowly read the Scripture passage several times.

MEDITATION

Take some time to reflect on the words and phrases in the text. Which words, phrases, or images speak most to you?

PRAYER

Offer the internalized passage back to God in the form of a personalized prayer of adoration, confession, renewal, petition, intercession, affirmation, or thanksgiving.

CONTEMPLATION

What word or image captures the spirit of the passage for you?

Take a few minutes to present yourself before God in silence and yieldedness. When your mind wanders, center yourself by returning to the spirit of the passage.

SCRIPTURE

I trusted in Christ when I heard the word of truth, the gospel of my salvation. Having believed, I was sealed in Him with the Holy Spirit of promise, who is a deposit guaranteeing my inheritance until the redemption of those who are God's possession, to the praise of His glory.
(Ephesians 1:13-14)

READING

Slowly read the Scripture passage several times.

MEDITATION

Take some time to reflect on the words and phrases in the text.
Which words, phrases, or images speak most to you?

PRAYER

Offer the internalized passage back to God in the form of a personalized prayer of adoration, confession, renewal, petition, intercession, affirmation, or thanksgiving.

CONTEMPLATION

What word or image captures the spirit of the passage for you?

Take a few minutes to present yourself before God in silence and yieldedness. When your mind wanders, center yourself by returning to the spirit of the passage.

SCRIPTURE

May God grant me, according to the riches of His glory, to be strengthened with power through His Spirit in my inner being, so that Christ may dwell in my heart through faith. And may I, being rooted and grounded in love, be able to comprehend with all the saints what is the width and length and height and depth of the love of Christ, and to know this love that surpasses knowledge, that I may be filled to all the fullness of God. (Ephesians 3:16-19)

READING

Slowly read the Scripture passage several times.

MEDITATION

Take some time to reflect on the words and phrases in the text. Which words, phrases, or images speak most to you?

PRAYER

Offer the internalized passage back to God in the form of a personalized prayer of adoration, confession, renewal, petition, intercession, affirmation, or thanksgiving.

CONTEMPLATION

What word or image captures the spirit of the passage for you?

Take a few minutes to present yourself before God in silence and yieldedness. When your mind wanders, center yourself by returning to the spirit of the passage.

SCRIPTURE

I do not want to grieve the Holy Spirit of God by whom I was sealed for the day of redemption. (Ephesians 4:30)

READING

Slowly read the Scripture passage several times.

MEDITATION

Take some time to reflect on the words and phrases in the text.
Which words, phrases, or images speak most to you?

PRAYER

Offer the internalized passage back to God in the form of a personalized prayer of adoration, confession, renewal, petition, intercession, affirmation, or thanksgiving.

CONTEMPLATION

What word or image captures the spirit of the passage for you?

Take a few minutes to present yourself before God in silence and yieldedness. When your mind wanders, center yourself by returning to the spirit of the passage.

SCRIPTURE

When the kindness and love of God my Savior appeared, He saved me, not by works of righteousness that I have done, but according to His mercy. He saved me through the washing of regeneration and renewal by the Holy Spirit whom He poured out on me abundantly through Jesus Christ my Savior, so that having been justified by His grace, I might become an heir according to the hope of eternal life. (Titus 3:4-7)

READING

Slowly read the Scripture passage several times.

MEDITATION

Take some time to reflect on the words and phrases in the text.
Which words, phrases, or images speak most to you?

PRAYER

Offer the internalized passage back to God in the form of a personalized prayer of adoration, confession, renewal, petition, intercession, affirmation, or thanksgiving.

CONTEMPLATION

What word or image captures the spirit of the passage for you?

Take a few minutes to present yourself before God in silence and yieldedness. When your mind wanders, center yourself by returning to the spirit of the passage.

SCRIPTURE

I have been chosen according to the foreknowledge of God the Father, in sanctification of the Spirit, for obedience to Jesus Christ and sprinkling of His blood; grace and peace are mine in abundance. (1 Peter 1:2)

READING

Slowly read the Scripture passage several times.

MEDITATION

Take some time to reflect on the words and phrases in the text. Which words, phrases, or images speak most to you?

PRAYER

Offer the internalized passage back to God in the form of a personalized prayer of adoration, confession, renewal, petition, intercession, affirmation, or thanksgiving.

CONTEMPLATION

What word or image captures the spirit of the passage for you?

Take a few minutes to present yourself before God in silence and yieldedness. When your mind wanders, center yourself by returning to the spirit of the passage.

SCRIPTURE

Those who obey Christ's commandments abide in Him, and He in them.
And this is how I know that He abides in me: by the Spirit whom He has
given me. (1 John 3:24)

READING

Slowly read the Scripture passage several times.

MEDITATION

Take some time to reflect on the words and phrases in the text.
Which words, phrases, or images speak most to you?

PRAYER

Offer the internalized passage back to God in the form of a personalized
prayer of adoration, confession, renewal, petition, intercession,
affirmation, or thanksgiving.

CONTEMPLATION

What word or image captures the spirit of the passage for you?

Take a few minutes to present yourself before God in silence and
yieldedness. When your mind wanders, center yourself by returning
to the spirit of the passage.

SCRIPTURE

I know that I abide in Christ, and He in me, because He has given me of His Spirit. (1 John 4:13)

READING

Slowly read the Scripture passage several times.

MEDITATION

Take some time to reflect on the words and phrases in the text. Which words, phrases, or images speak most to you?

PRAYER

Offer the internalized passage back to God in the form of a personalized prayer of adoration, confession, renewal, petition, intercession, affirmation, or thanksgiving.

CONTEMPLATION

What word or image captures the spirit of the passage for you?

Take a few minutes to present yourself before God in silence and yieldedness. When your mind wanders, center yourself by returning to the spirit of the passage.

$\mathcal{W}$HERE TO GO FROM HERE

I trust that this ninety-day process has been meaningful and spiritually nourishing for you. Now that you have completed *The Trinity: A Journal*, you should go back and read through the comments and prayers you have recorded. As you do this, be sure to mark the journal entries that strongly resonate with your spirit.

As I mentioned at the end of the introduction, it would be especially helpful for you to go through this process a second time and visit each of these passages once again. You will discover new things in the Scripture texts that you did not see the first time through. Use a different color of ink for your journal comments each time you revisit a passage.

I also encourage you to use the other journals in this *Reflections* series. *Sacred Readings: A Journal* presents ninety Scripture texts from Numbers through Revelation that are particularly well-suited to the process of sacred reading. These texts range from one to several verses, and they are arranged in biblical sequence to attune you to the flow of progressive revelation.

Historic Creeds: A Journal moves through three historic creeds of the faith (the Apostles' Creed, the Nicene Creed, and the Athanasian Creed) and relates each element of these creeds to a Scripture text for sacred reading.

The Psalms: A Journal will enhance your devotional life as you meditate on and pray ninety selections from the book of Psalms back to God.

ABOUT THE AUTHOR

DR. KENNETH BOA is the president of Reflections Ministries. He has authored many books, including *Pursuing Wisdom* and *The Art of Living Well* (both NavPress), and is a contributing editor to the *Open Bible*, the *Promise Keeper's Men's Study Bible*, and the *Leadership Bible*. Dr. Boa earned a bachelor's degree from Case Institute of Technology, a master's degree in theology from Dallas Theological Seminary, and doctoral degrees from both New York University and the University of Oxford. He resides in Atlanta, Georgia.

Kenneth Boa writes a free monthly teaching letter called Reflections. If you would like to be on the mailing list, call: 800-DRAW NEAR (800-372-9632).

CULTIVATE A PASSION FOR CHRIST

The Psalms
Read through ninety select psalms and learn the ancient spiritual disciplines of contemplative reading, reflection, and meditative prayer that will bring you a more passionate relationship with God.
The Psalms (Kenneth Boa) $10

Sacred Readings
Are you seeking meaningful time with God? This journal will help you intensify your relationship with Him as you study the sacred Scriptures of the faith.
Sacred Readings (Kenneth Boa) $10

Historic Creeds
A number of historic statements, including the Apostles' Creed, will help you develop a better understanding of the truths upon which Christ's church was built.
Historic Creeds (Kenneth Boa) $10

Get your copies today at your local bookstore, visit our website at www.navpress.com, or call (800) 366-7788 and ask for offer **#6117** or a FREE catalog of NavPress products.

NAVPRESS
BRINGING TRUTH TO LIFE
www.navpress.com